Time Management

A Step-by-step Guide To Improve Your Productivity, Time Management, And Self-discipline So You Can Achieve Your Personal And Professional Goals

(The Complete Guide To The Most Powerful Strategies, Abilities, And Methods For Managing Your Time)

Logan Hester

TABLE OF CONTENT

Introduction 1

Instructions On How To Manage Time For Novices 10

Applications That Increase Productivity Are A Bonus. 16

Fundamentals Of Time Management 21

It Is Important To Steer Clear Of Interruptions And Diversions. 28

How To Become More Productive While Also Become More Organized 39

Take Control Of Your Procrastination 44

Performer Who Can Say, "I Can Perform Well, Even When I'm Under A Lot Of Pressure." 47

Time For Sleeping And Time For Working Out 55

There Are So Many Things To Do, But So Little Time. 59

The Rule Of 21 Days To Overcome Your Tendency To Put Things Off 66

Strategy Formulation And Execution 80

The Study Of Patterns That Lead To Achievement 90

The Benefits And Drawbacks Of Multitasking When Managing Your Time 100

Quickly Adapt To Any Changes 107

The Management Of Time And Its Tools 115

You Should Prioritise The Management Of Your Energy Rather Than Your Time. 121

Putting Too Many Goals In Front Of You Might Be Distracting 136

The Importance Of Managing Time Effectively 143

Having A Good Handle On Time Management 150

Productivity-Boosting Patterns You Should Adopt 159

Introduction

Your purchase of this book, "Time Management: Destroy Deadlines, Complete Projects, and Control Your Habits for Less Laziness and Increased Productivity," is very appreciated. Please accept our warmest greetings. In this book, we will discuss a variety of strategies that might help us better manage our time, as well as the implications of doing nothing at all. The fact of the matter is that there is not just one thing that we can do that will make us excellent time managers; rather, there are a lot of things that we can do that, when combined, will bring about this result for us. When it comes to managing our time effectively, the activities we engage in are much more important than the quantity of free time we regain. The purpose of effective time management is to enable us to do high-leverage work at the best possible level in the shortest amount of time, and this is why it is so important. Many individuals at work waste their time by putting off critical work, failing to set priorities, and concentrating their efforts on less significant but nevertheless time-consuming activities such as responding to email. In this book, you will discover why multitasking is a terrible practise and why it should be avoided at all costs. In addition to this, we will go over some of the most prevalent errors in poor time management and how we may improve them. In chapter 5, we will also talk about how you can set yourself up for a productive day by getting off to a good start with a positive morning routine and how this can help set the tone for the rest of your day. Chapter 5 will go more into what a morning ritual is and how everyone has some type of a morning routine. If you are unclear on what a morning ritual is, then you should read chapter 5. Because of this, it is imperative that we purposefully build one to suit our preferences. If you have a look at the phrase "morning ritual," then you'll have a decent sense of what the meaning of this term is. However, the definition is very straightforward on its own.

The following are some things you can do right now to enhance your abilities in time management and allow yourself more time to accomplish the things that are most important to you. The first thing you need to do is get rid of your television set. If you own a television or watch it on a regular basis, the amount of time you spend in front of it each evening will rapidly add up. When added up over the course of the next few days, weeks, and months, it will take up a significant amount of your valuable time. Do not make it a habit to partake in it every evening or make it a regular activity since doing so is an efficient approach to shorten the duration of the waiting period. It's possible that in the years to come, you may find yourself looking back on your life and being astounded by how swiftly it passed, wondering what you would have done differently if you could change the past. If you don't learn to wean yourself off of your dependence on the TV, you'll have your TV to thank for that. The next step is to keep track of the amount of time you spend working. By this, I mean that you should take regular breaks and organise your work into chunks of intense working periods that last for 90 minutes followed by 10 minutes of relaxation. When you look back at the end of the day at what you've achieved, you'll notice that working in this manner has given you more time to concentrate on your objectives, given you more energy after rest, and allowed you to get more work done in an efficient manner. To get the intended effect in your life, you need exercise on both the morning and the evening of each day. This is a step that I have not yet taken for myself, but it is one that will bring about the desired result. Exercise is what releases energy, and it provides us the inner power to keep going when things become difficult so that we can achieve our objectives. This may seem counterintuitive, but it's true. If you work out twice a day, you will be able to tap into secret reserves of energy that you did not know you had accessible to you. If you go to the gym in the evening, there is a good probability that you will attend at a time when the gym is full with other persons who have done their job for the day and are aiming to relieve tension after having a productive day. The next step is to engage in public activities during times that are not considered to be peak times. Find out when the gym is less crowded, and avoid going at times when it is likely to be more crowded, since this will increase the amount of time you spend waiting. Another piece of advice that may be followed is to avoid holding dozens upon dozens of meetings on a regular basis. Meetings have a function, but holding too many of them can have an impact that is detrimental to the task that your team is attempting to complete. You should try to keep them to a minimum as much as possible so that you may spend your time working on the most essential activities that will lead to the greatest forward movement. Even while meetings may be urgent a good portion of the time, this does not mean that they are always vital. Next, we have a routine that is more difficult but unquestionably extremely rewarding, and that is to get up at five in the morning every day. The military has this training regiment for a reason, but if you want to take command of your day, try waking up at this time to get more done so that you may take care of your life. A statement made by Stefan Pylarinos that reads, "If you're behind on your goals, dreams, and bills, wake up earlier," is one that I agree with. Avoiding distractions is another piece of advice that is covered in further detail later on in the book. In this day and age, distractions have only grown in number and have gotten more effective at diverting our focus away from what is really essential. Find a place where you won't be easily distracted, however the optimal setting may vary depending on the specifics of your situation. If you work in a shared office space, it may be worthwhile to ask your coworkers to leave you alone for a few hours so that you can get some important work done. This will give you the opportunity to focus on getting things done. If you perform most or all of your work from home, it may be worthwhile to invest in converting a room into an office space. The goal is to create a location that is distinct from both your work area and your play space. Don't combine your job with your pleasure. If you have any downtime during your commute, you can decide to use it to further your education. Depending on the length of your commute, you'll want to make the most of the time you spend travelling, and audio books are becoming an increasingly common way to do so. If your commute is thirty minutes each way, it adds up to an hour per day, five hours per week, and twenty hours per month. If you put that time towards useful endeavours, you might gain an extra day of knowledge in a little over a month. It is a commonly held belief in the self-development business that who you spend your time with is who you become. Even if you consider yourself to be quite a positive person, spending time with negative individuals will in some way pull you down. Another sensible thing to do is to avoid spending time with negative people. This is because it is a widely held belief that who you spend your time with is who you become. They'll also sap your energy, which is energy that might be better spent finishing critical work or making forward towards your objectives. Last but not least, consider contracting out work that does not have to be performed by you personally. If you are unable to do certain duties to a high and consistent degree, then there is no need for you to undertake the work yourself. If it isn't what you're being paid for, you can easily locate websites online or individuals with that specific ability who are willing to execute the work for you, and the cost is usually quite reasonable.

According to a survey, one in every three persons who are employed has stress due to their inboxes on a daily basis. This is a problem for many of us who are employed. Emails are low leverage jobs, which means that they are often insignificant for the long term. Because of this, we need to make a speedy choice on what to do with the email as soon as it is received. Don't be late because every second you're late is a second of time that you'll never get back. Here are four choices you can make right now to relieve the stress caused by email. If you have ever registered to a newsletter or website, then there is a good probability that you will get daily automatic emails from them. These emails will take up space in both your junk mail folder and your primary inbox. The first step is to remove these emails. It will be difficult to distinguish the automated emails from the rest of the messages in the inbox. As a result, it is probable that you can remove half of the emails that you have right now. The next option available to you is to identify emails that need immediate attention and can be dealt with in a relatively short amount of time. When you come across these time-sensitive emails, resolve to deal with them as soon as possible. Delegate tasks to other people if you discover when reading the emails that your own expertise is not well-suited to deal with the inquiry. In this case, it may be desirable to pass the email on to someone who has the appropriate knowledge to deal with the query. If you discover that you spend an excessive amount of time on emails, which is a typical problem in the workplace, then you should put the email to the side for a later time. This brings us to the last choice, which is to delay the email. Ideally, once you have finished all of the jobs that have the highest leverage initially.

When we are productive and get things done, we have less stress, and when this occurs, we conveniently become more productive. It's almost like a self-fulfilling cycle; the more effectively we manage our time, the more time we have available to us. Although it can seem counterintuitive to spend time studying about it, I can guarantee that reading this book will be worthwhile if you put the information it contains into practise. I have high hopes that readers would come away from reading this book with a better understanding of the significance of time, the value of time, and the methods by which it may be effectively handled to achieve success in all aspects of life. It's possible that a person doesn't have their own unique personality if they spend their time engaging in things that are either pointless or useless. Take Tony Robins as an example; he sees himself as a life coach, a motivational speaker, an author, a giver, and basically as someone who is bringing back to mankind in as many positive ways as possible. He is driven to discover methods that will permanently improve the lives of other people. This persona that he carries about with him is what gives him the motivation to assist as many people as he possibly can. You won't catch him squandering any of his time on anything that isn't related to his interests.

Instructions On How To Manage Time For Novices

The process of planning, organising, and exercising control over the amount of time spent on certain tasks in order to raise one's level of productivity, efficiency, or effectiveness is referred to as time management. Each of us has just 24 hours in a day to achieve all of the responsibilities and objectives that we have set for ourselves for that day. Time is a finite resource. Effective time management is the process of making better use of the time you have available to you by determining what you do with it, how you spend it, and keeping your attention on the activity you have selected to do. recognising that successful time management is about good behaviours, patience, and perseverance rather than having extra minutes or hours in a day is the key to excellent time management. The secret to good time management rests in recognising this.

Why It's Important to Have an Effective Time Management Strategy to Practise

Management of one's time is of the utmost significance whether one is at job, school, or at home. The following are some important advantages of practising effective time management:

One, an Increase in Spare Time

You can have the impression that you have an excessive amount of work to finish but not enough time to do it. If, on the other hand, you organise your tasks, put them on a timetable, and ensure that you do each one within the allotted amount of time, you won't need to spend time deciding what to do.

You won't waste much time transitioning from one task to another since you are familiar with what comes next. If you are able to complete your responsibilities and duties in the allotted amount of time, you will have more spare time to devote to activities that bring you joy. You are free to take use of this spare time to unwind, engage in activities of your choosing, and rest.

However, if you fail to practise effective time management, the chores you have to do will wind up taking more time than is necessary, which will not only exhaust you but also leave you with no spare time to accomplish the things that you like.

2: Improved Capability to Decide The Capability of Making

It is quite simple to make the incorrect choice when you are truly feeling as if you are pushed for time, even though you need to make a decision, since it is very easy to make the wrong selection without thoroughly evaluating the many possibilities when you are in this situation. On the other hand, if you practise effective time management because you have planned, you will have a sense of peace, which will alleviate the strain that is sometimes brought on by the perception that you do not have enough time to do the tasks that need to be completed. In the absence of this pressure, you will be able to make deliberate decisions and devote your time to doing things that are both beneficial and significant.

3. Decreased Amounts of Stress

Because you will know how long it will take to complete an activity and the best technique to employ to accomplish a task within its given time and deadline, you will be able to prevent the stress that comes with personal difficulties or frictions with others when you regulate your time. This is because you will know how long it will take to complete an activity. You will have decided what you want to do for the day, ranked the importance of various activities or tasks, and crafted an in-depth plan that outlines how you expect to complete each activity or job.

At the end of the day, you will be able to minimise the strain and feeling of being overwhelmed that comes from having duties that are either not completed or completed inadequately.

4. Encourages the Development of Self-Control

Self-discipline is an important skill that has a significant impact on your life. If you have a strategy for managing your time, you will plan for every minute of the day, and you won't wind up spending time on unnecessary tasks like reading the newest celebrity news since you will have prepared for every minute.

You will be able to successfully prevent procrastination if you have a good time management strategy since it will guide and motivate you when you feel like skipping a task that has to be completed. You will be aware of your objectives as well as the rewards or advantages that come from achieving your goals; as a result, you will feel the drive to finish each activity or work within the allotted time without leaving any activity or task undone.

Applications That Increase Productivity Are A Bonus.

There are a lot of helpful programmes that are available on the internet and in mobile app stores that may make your life and job a lot less difficult. Here are some of them.

This ingenious piece of software, known as Nozbe, is capable of pulling data from dozens of widely used applications found on the internet and enabling you to create and manage tasks for each of those applications. It's fantastic for helping you better manage both your time and your tasks. There is a free version, a premium version, and versions for mobile apps to choose from.

This software lets you monitor all of your goals in one place, see all of your data in one view, establish milestones and "levels" to complete, contains a habit tracker that helps to break bad habits, and tells you how many times in a week you achieved your goal with the average goal tracker. Stridesapp is available for iOS and Android devices.

Stayfocused — This may help you remain focussed on work duties by restricting the amount of time you can spend on websites like Facebook. This frees up more time for you to complete other job-related responsibilities. You will not be able to access these websites for the remainder of the day once you have used up the time allotted to you for using them. You have the option to set an allowance. You have control over which websites are banned or permitted, as well as the length of time for which they are prohibited. You also have the ability to choose which days the plugin will be active. (Take note: this only works for those who use Google Chrome.)

Momentum is a feature that enables the creation of a customised dashboard that includes to-do lists, objectives for the day, and motivational quotations. (Take note: this only works for those who use Google Chrome.)

Asana (https://asana.com) This is a web-based tool that assists you in managing tasks, projects, and more especially teams. If you work in a team or manage a team, this may assist you in allocating and monitoring tasks, as well as remote working and tracking progress.

Rescuetime is a programme that enables users to monitor how they spend their time in order to improve their decision-making around how their time should be allocated to achieve their objectives.

This application compiles news from a variety of sources and presents it in the form of digestible chunks of data that are simple to read while on the go. As a result, it helps you save time while still ensuring that you remain informed.

This desktop programme, known as Time Doctor, is a time tracking and time management software that enables the user to keep better track of time and do more on a daily basis.

Klock is a piece of project management software that provides you with a bird's-eye perspective of the several endeavours on which you are now engaged.

Fundamentals Of Time Management

Time is one of the most essential components of a person's existence. Time once gone can never be gained again, which is why it is essential to be aware of how you spend your days and how you spend your time. When you lose something, there is no way to get it back again. The sad thing about time is that it may fly by in the blink of an eye, leaving you exactly where you started off. Learning how to manage your time effectively is essential if you want to make the most of the 24 hours in a day that you have available to you.

Remaining stuck in the past

Many individuals are stuck in the past because they have allowed so much time to pass without making any progress in their lives, and as a result, they have little choice but to dwell on the past. Living in the past is a highly harmful habit because it prevents you from moving on in life and from experiencing the enjoyment that you deserve after accomplishing something, both of which are things that you deserve. To live in the past is to constantly compare and contrast the things you have done in the past with the things you have not done. In the majority of situations, you will never feel satisfied, particularly if you have not been very successful in the past. This is especially true if you have not done something really noteworthy. You spend your life ruminating on ways in which things might be improved, rather than moving on from your mistakes of the past and making the most of the opportunities that are now available to you.

Being present in the here and now

Everyone should think of the current moment as a gift since now is the time to put things right in their lives, and this moment should be appreciated as such. You may not have accomplished much in the past, but now that the present has here, you should be able to alter all of that and make significant progress towards a life filled with tremendous satisfaction.

There is a lot that can be altered in the here and now. You have the power right now to alter the perception others have of you, even if that perception is that you are a person who is considered to be lethargic and unable to complete a certain work. The present is also the time to experiment with new activities that you would have been too afraid to do in the past. There is a lot of time, and if you are able to effectively manage your time, you should be able to look back into the past and see how much you have accomplished with your life. If there is a lot of time, then you should be able to look back into the past.

When you effectively manage your time, you will be able to organise yourself and plan exactly how you will divide the time that you have available among the many things that you want to do in a given day, week, month, or even an entire year.

If you are able to effectively manage your time, you will always be able to work intelligently. You have come to the conclusion that working smarter, rather than working extremely hard, is the way to get everything done before the end of the day. It is not necessary to put in as many hours at work in order to accomplish as much as you can in a single day. As soon as you have a good strategy for your chores, you can start working intelligently, which means that you may accomplish a great deal in a relatively short amount of time.

When there is too much work to do and not enough time in the day or the week, effective time management may work wonders. You make a plan for what to do first and what to do after a specific amount of time, and by the time the length of time that you planned for has passed, you will have completed everything on your list. Because you are not able to perform as successfully as you should be because you have not planned for your time, you are likely to experience a great deal of stress.

Is it an easy goal to reach?

There are a total of 24 hours in a day, and although everyone has them, some individuals are able to pack a lot into those hours while others are unable to get anything done at all. This is entirely due to the fact that some individuals are better able to organise and manage their time than others. There are people in this world who are great achievers, and they are able to successfully manage their time so that they may perform more efficiently. Anyone may improve their quality of life by doing a great deal each day if they have the knowledge, skills, and strategies necessary for effective time management.

Therefore, effective time management is quite simple to obtain. Simply shifting your attention from working hard to working smart can allow you to accomplish greater outcomes each and every day.

The following is a list of benefits that may be attained by effective management of one's time:

A solid professional reputation earned by one's efficiency and resourcefulness in producing outcomes

Because you can get so much done in such a short amount of time, you will experience far less stress.

More findings, despite the restricted amount of time

There is so much time that might be spent on other things, such as one's own development.

Consequences of failing to properly manage one's time

People who are unable to effectively manage their time will consistently be late for everything. They run the risk of missing out on a multitude of possibilities in life due to the fact that no one wants to collaborate with someone who cannot perform within the specified amount of time.

Due to the fact that they attempt to do everything at once, they do not have an effective workflow.

The low quality of their work is due to the fact that, rather than concentrating on the quality of their job, they are working very hard to achieve their deadlines.

They have a negative reputation in their professional community, which might prevent them from advancing in their chosen field.

They are always agitated because they are unsure of what they should do first and what they should do last. They constantly consider the amount of labour to be excessive, even though it is feasible to do. Because it takes so long for them to get started, they consistently miss their deadlines.

Planning your job may make it seem more manageable and straightforward to carry out, which is an essential component of effective time management. Time management is a skill that has to be mastered if one want to work more efficiently and effectively and to accomplish more on a daily basis.

It Is Important To Steer Clear Of Interruptions And Diversions.

Our capacity to suppress disruptions and stay focused on the task at hand is essential to efficient time management. The overarching purpose of all of the different time management principles is to educate us on how to get more done in less time by minimising the number of unneeded interruptions in our daily lives.

The secret to being more productive and successful in life is very apparent: steer clear of distractions and focus only on the activities that are most important to you.

During the course of my work on a significant project, I came to the conclusion that it is impossible for me to complete it without being disrupted. The internet merely starts to run more slowly, or my laptop starts having problems. If I do not run into any technological problems, my supervisor will give me some paperwork to perform that is always time-sensitive and has to be completed by a certain date. When I am interrupted twice or more, all possibility of me becoming inspired is eliminated.

You may save many hours over the course of a week by effectively managing these interruptions. It will save you both time and effort. A fresh way of thinking is necessary for management on this level.

In his book The 4-Hour Workweek, Tim Ferriss advised his readers to "beg for forgiveness, rather than ask for permission." This strategy results in substantial time savings. For instance, you should apologise to your coworkers and let them know that you will not be able to check your email first thing in the morning. They need to get in touch with you through phone in the event that there is a critical situation. Inform your coworkers that you are working quickly in order to meet the deadline. "Only get in touch with me if the assignment cannot be put off until the following day."

Interruptions that are typical during working hours

1. Texts and Electronic Mail

2. Electronic and Social Media

3. Interruptions Caused by Customers

4. Phone Calls to Individuals

5. Requests at the eleventh hour

6. Unanticipated Confrontations

7. Distractions caused by television, music, and other noises

The following are some extremely significant pointers to keep in mind while attempting to prevent interruptions:

1. Limit yourself to checking your email just twice each day.

If you are anything like me, then each day you will be inundated with hundreds of emails. You will never have enough time to read all of these emails, therefore the work at hand is to prioritise which ones are most essential and then move on.

It should become a routine for you to only check your email twice a day. You also have the option of employing a virtual assistant to check the mailbox on your behalf. They are able to screen your incoming emails for you. You will be immediately alerted in the event that a significant job demands urgent attention thanks to this method.

2. Make effective use of available technological resources.

Have you ever noticed that there is a button labelled "Do not disturb" on your phone? You'll find the same button on your own personal Skype account. Both Facebook and Gmail allow you to modify your "Mood Status" at any time. Please use these buttons. Utilise the tools and resources available to you. It is not essential to go back to each and every customer and friend in a timely manner. Getting things done that are vital at the time they need to be done is an important job. Your life has more value than everything else in the world. Conduct your life in accordance with your values. Do not let things like the phone, Facebook, instant messaging, and other such technologies control your life.

3. Prepare in advance

You should never go to your workstation without first having a complete list of tasks to do. Before beginning work on a project, you are required to create a plan of action. It's easy to spend an hour just by greeting the day with "Good morning" and looking at a blank computer. When you plan ahead, you might get an idea of how the day will go. Begin with the project that will be the most challenging and will also be the most significant. The tasks that are most essential to you should take up the majority of your time.

Imagine for a moment that you are toiling away all by yourself in an exotic forest. Your internet connection is working just fine. The PC and its attachments all seem to be operational. The environment is calm, and the progress made on the task is impressive. You are completely certain that the task at hand will be finished within the next hour. You are hit by a wave of thirst all of a sudden. You realise that you are completely alone in the forest, and there is no way for you to contact anybody else.

As was shown, there is no section of the planet in which you would not experience any disruptions. It is advisable to set aside some time for things that can't be predicted to happen.

4. Comparing Action and Reaction

Acquire command of your own life. Take command of your thoughts. It is required of you to act in this manner. Get things done so you can stop wasting time. Create a plan to ensure that you make the most of the time you have available. On the other hand, there is a distinction to be made between actions and reactions. Certain individuals have exceptional ability to concentrate, allowing them to complete their task despite the presence of a variety of distractions. Switching between the various forms of labour is not possible for other persons. Before moving on to the next task, they have to finish the one they are now working on.

It is essential to have an understanding of your point of view. Make an effort to strike a healthy balance. Learn to comprehend your own feelings. Frustration in the workplace may do real harm to both your reputation and your productivity.

Take a moment to collect your thoughts, calm yourself, and proceed with caution.

Office Proficiency

Here is a list of ten office skills that you may use to make better use of your time and save a minute each day. You are not going to make the mistake of thinking that you can put them on in two steps. Be on the lookout for one activity that you may start performing now, this week, or this month to further strengthen your office abilities, and keep an eye out for it.

Time-Saving Tip No. 11: Provide Support to Customers Via Video

Respond to inquiries about customer service through video. This is dependent on the breadth of your ability, and in my experience, it took longer to make a video than it did to figure out a response to the question. On the other hand, if you are excellent at being impromptu, if you are good at chatting on the phone or if you are good at talking in person, it may be a better use of your time to respond to things via the medium of video.

Whether it's with ScreenFlow or Camtasia, or even with jingproject.com, that is a free piece of software that will allow you to create short screen capture recordings, grab a USB headset (I use any USB headset from Logitech), and answer questions as video. You may do this in a number of ways.

Put a stop to using your brain.

Your mind was in the "off" position when you made the decisions that turned out to be the best for your life. This is due to the fact that when you are confronted with a challenging decision, rather of focusing on the choice itself, your attention is drawn to the critical voice in your head that is trying to convince you that an option is not viable.

What ends up happening is that you get paralysed by fear, and as a result, you wind up not doing anything... this is a certain strategy for fizzling out. I was trying to work myself out of it for the ten minutes leading up to the time when I gave my boss notice that I was leaving my usual daily job. I was able to come up with hundreds of explanations for why it wouldn't work, and many more excuses for why I should back out.

I accessed my ledger on my own computer just before heading to the office of my supervisor. I had a look at the enormous balance in my investment money, which was that amount and nothing more. I was thinking about how easy it is to pivot as I walked to the office of my boss when I suddenly remembered that number. My thoughts ultimately triumphed over my emotions. The most challenging aspect, as it turned out, was just entering his office. When I sat down, I was given the opportunity to inform him that I would be quitting, which was not an issue at all.

It's the equivalent of asking someone out on a date or bidding someone goodbye for the last time. It is challenging to get started, but once you do, you can't believe how close you were to missing out on the opportunity.

Turn off your mind and get things done before you have the chance to think your way out of the situation.

How To Become More Productive While Also Become More Organized

Just because you're good at managing your time doesn't guarantee you're also productive. To clarify, what I mean is that I may schedule two days to perform a work that only requires a half day to complete. The thing that really counts is getting your life organised so that you may complete more responsibilities and realise more objectives. After that, you'll have more time on your hands to devote to the activities that really excite you.

In order to make ourselves organised, we need to take care of everything that is around us. When we are at work, we are required to handle a variety of tasks, including emails, phone calls, meetings, presentations, and so on. When we are at home, we are obligated to take care of chores, members of the family, children, or relatives... etc. We are literally occupied with something for the whole of each and every day.

How do we prioritise the many issues that need our attention? What should our top priority be?

It is necessary for us to divide the jobs into these four groups.

#1: Critically Important and Time-Critical #2: Critically Important but Not Time-Critical

#3: Not Important, but Urgent #4: Neither Urgent nor Important

You have undoubtedly read in some of the previous books that you have read that we should always deal with things that are not urgent but are vital. In the event that you are not already aware with this, allow me to provide a brief summary below.

Why should we prioritise the jobs that are not urgent but important above the duties that are both urgent and important?

You will discover that you have the mentality of a firefighter if you are always juggling duties that are both critical and urgent. When there is a fire, the situation is critical and time-sensitive, and you have to rush to put out the flames. This sort of job may often put you under stress, which, in the long run, will have an impact on both your productivity and your health.

When you begin working on activities that are significant but are not urgent, you do not have a precise deadline in front of you. You are not under any pressure to complete this assignment, which enables you to give your whole attention to the work at hand. In addition, if you consistently work on projects that are important but not urgent, you will progressively have less and fewer jobs that are "urgent and important" for you to deal with. This is because you will have previously completed a task before it became imperative for you to do so.

When I first read it, the idea that went through my head was, "This is a fantastic principle." On the other hand, I was unable to find out how to precisely classify activities, and I discovered that certain jobs may be assigned to more than one group. By using what I've learned in both theory and practise, I've found that adopting a 3W strategy yields much superior outcomes.

The 3W system is a system that consists of three phases. Simply following these three processes is all that is required whether you are processing stuff, thoughts, or tasks:

In reality, the three stages consist of three questions that you pose to yourself.

1. What are the steps that come after this?

2. At what point should this be carried out?

3. Where should I put it away?

When you take a job from one of your collection stations, you are obligated to provide a response to the following question: "What's the next step?"

"Can I do it right now?"

If you are able to do the following step in the procedure right now, then you should. In the event that you are unable to do the subsequent step, you will need to provide a response to the second question, which is "When should this be done?"

When you have the solution, go ahead and schedule the assignment. After you have determined "when," the next question you need to answer is "where do I store it?" Include the activity on your list of things to accomplish if it must be completed by the following day. Putting the work on your calendar is a good idea if it has to be completed in the next week. You have completed the job that you were working on at this time.

Take Control Of Your Procrastination.

Procrastination is defined as "being slow or late about doing something that should be done; delaying doing something until a later time because you do not want to do it, because you are lazy, apathetic, etc." This definition comes directly from the dictionary.

When you are under the influence of procrastination, you are most likely engaging in a kind of failed self-regulation that is characterised by illogical delays in the completion of tasks. Or, in certain instances, they are searching for the rush of excitement that comes with the tension that comes with the heat of the moment, when the job has to be accomplished as quickly as possible. You are moving your workload into the Important / Urgent quadrant of the Eisenhower Matrix on purpose in this instance, although in a more typical scenario, it would have been located in the Important / Not Urgent quadrant of the matrix.

Take, for instance, the fact that you have a job assignment for which the due date is the next week. It would seem that there is sufficient time to do the task. excluding someone who is a chronic procrastinator. He will continue to put off beginning the task until the deadline is really close, as in "next day" close. Even if the issue is entirely due to oneself, she or he will make every effort to push back the deadline for a couple of extra days if at all feasible.

The vast majority of professionals will, deliberately or unwittingly, enter the domain of procrastination at some time in their professional lives. However, they may not be aware of the appropriate procedures to emerge from this area successfully. Procrastination is something that affects a lot of people, regardless of whether they are running a business or working as freelancers. It is more common to see procrastination as an issue of managing one's emotions than as a problem with managing one's time. I don't fully agree with the statement that as soon as you remove procrastination from your job, your calendar will become more transparent, your to-do list will stop being flipped upside down all the time, and you will regain your sense of composure in your work environment.

If you have an issue and you want to find a solution to it, the first step is to recognise that you have a problem. This is true for every situation. The specialists on procrastination have categorised people who engage in the behaviour according to one of four distinct categories, so that things will be simpler for all of us. Can you empathise with any one of them?

Performer Who Can Say, "I Can Perform Well, Even When I'm Under A Lot Of Pressure."

Some people in business have the misconception that they can do well even when they are under intense pressure. These individuals prefer to operate under a time constraint, which forces them to concentrate by reducing the amount of time they have at their disposal to complete a job. As a result, they are better able to concentrate on the work at hand. Perfectionism is the driving force behind procrastination for many people who suffer from this illness. They believe that if they do a work on time, it would not be able to live up to their standards. However, this is not the case. Others see it as little more than a chance to revert to previously established routines. Putting this much pressure on oneself is not a good idea under any circumstances, and it is definitely not sustainable. This is true even if the task at hand is completed quickly and well.

Since getting started would likely be the most difficult part of the project for you, one solution to this issue would be to reverse the process and schedule a precise day for when you will begin work on it. You may relieve a significant portion of the strain that you are putting on yourself by shifting your emphasis from the time that you expect to finish a job to the time that you intend to start working on it.

Prepare a Detailed Written Plan Every great manager is an excellent planner. They use both simple and complex means in order to achieve each of their primary and secondary goals. When a new project comes across their desk, they take the time to think through exactly what it is that they want to achieve, and then they write down an organised list, in sequence, of every step that is essential for the completion of the project. This process is repeated whenever a new project comes across their desk.

One minute spent planning should be equivalent to ten minutes spent carrying out the plan. This is the general rule. You will get a return on your personal energy of 1,000 percent if you take the time to consider on paper about anything you need to do before you begin work. This equates to ten minutes saved for every minute that you invest in planning your job in the first place.

When you have a good understanding of your objective, the next step is to write down everything you can think of that is necessary to do in order to reach that objective. You should continue to add new items to the list whenever you think of them in order to finish compiling it. Sequence and priority should both be considered while organising your list.

First, when you organise by sequence, you make a list of activities in the order that they should be completed, beginning with the very first step and ending with the very last step before the completion of the goal or project.

The second step is to establish priorities for these items, keeping in mind that twenty percent of the items on your list will be responsible for eighty percent of the total value and significance of everything you do. The process of setting priorities enables you to continue concentrating on the tasks and activities that are most important to you without becoming sidetracked.

The things that matter most must never be dependent on the things that matter least. This is an absolute must.

Make it a habit to review your ideas on a regular basis, and do so in particular if you encounter frustration or resistance of any kind. When you get new information or feedback, be ready to adjust your plans accordingly and have an open mind.

Keep in mind that practically every plan has at least one flaw, no matter how big or how minor. Maintain a constant search for them. If you review your plans on a daily basis, you will be able to generate fresh concepts, points of view, and insights into how you might do the task more quickly and effectively than you would have originally thought possible.

Every failure can be traced back to one thing: action taken without proper forethought. Resist the urge to put your plans into action before giving them careful consideration and planning in advance.

Making a Game Plan to Achieve Your Goals

Clarity is maybe the single most important concept in relation to attaining success of any type.

People that are successful have a crystal clear idea of who they are and what they want out of life, and this clarity extends to every aspect of their existence. People that are successful not only have their goals written down, but they also have a documented plan of action that they adhere to on a daily basis.

After you have established a more ambitious objective for yourself and/or your company, ask yourself the following questions:

Where do you stand in terms of the challenges and roadblocks that you need to overcome in order to realise your ambitions? Why haven't you already accomplished what you set out to do? What is it that is stopping you? What is it that's stopping you? What difficulties must you overcome in order to achieve your objective in the long run, and what challenges must you solve in order to do so? What are the 20 percent of the difficulties you need to address that account for 80 percent of the obstacle between you and your goal? Among all the problems you need to tackle, what are the 20 percent of the problems that account for the most difficulty?

What more knowledge, skills, or information do you need in order to accomplish your objective or bring your project to a successful conclusion? You should always keep in mind the proverb that says, "Whatever got you to where you are today is not enough to get you any further." Where can you get the additional knowledge and skills that you need in order to accomplish what you set out to do? Is it possible to purchase or rent the necessary information or knowledge? Do you feel that in order for you to reach your full potential in your work, you need to work on developing new skills in yourself? Which pieces of information are most important to you when it comes to reaching your objective and making the best decisions along the way?

Who are the individuals, communities, or organisations whose assistance and collaboration you will need in order to realise your objective? Sometimes, a single person may provide you with ideas and inspiration or open doors for you, assisting you in doing much more than you previously believed was feasible for you to do. It is for the same reason that many business persons get into joint ventures and strategic alliances with their competitors in order to provide products and services to each other's customers that they do not already offer. Specifically, this is the reason why this is done.

Who is the most important person among all those who can assist you in achieving your objective, given the many people who can do so? What might you possibly give up in return to earn this person's assistance and cooperation in order to make progress towards the crucial objectives you have set for yourself?

People who plan out their actions in great detail before beginning even the most important projects in business and in the world around us are the ones that successfully execute such projects. You should create written plans for both yourself and your company, and then you should adhere to those plans as closely as possible until they are realised.

Time For Sleeping And Time For Working Out

Time spent relaxing is an essential component in optimising the productive cycle you follow. It is essential that you never go without breaks in between your job periods. This is due to the fact that getting enough rest is necessary in order for your mind to unwind. As a result, establish a regular time for each of your work intervals, and then schedule a regular break in between each set of progressively shorter intervals.

Additionally, there is a proverb that says a healthy mind resides in a healthy body. Therefore, maintaining a consistent exercise routine is also very important. However, most individuals do not devote a sufficient amount of time to their workout routine. You need to take precautions to ensure that you do not make that error.

Why is physical activity so important for the mental health?

Exercising regularly has been shown to provide a number of health benefits, including assisting with weight loss, lowering blood pressure, maintaining healthy sugar levels, and a host of other advantages. However, relatively few individuals are aware that regular physical activity may also aid to enhance one's mental health in addition to their physical health.

The capacity of the brain to store memories and the speed and quality of mental processes are both helped along by regular exercise, which is a scientific truth that has been proven. This is because physical activity encourages the production of growth factors in the brain, which is one of the benefits of exercising. Chemicals known as growth factors play an important role in ensuring that brain cells continue to remain in good condition. These factors also contribute to the development of new blood arteries in the brain.

In addition, physical activity has been shown to boost both mood and quality of sleep. These aspects serve as an extra booster to the productivity of the one who experiences them. Therefore, it should come as no surprise that engaging in regular physical activity may be of great assistance in preserving mental health.

Your productivity will greatly rise if you exercise on a consistent basis. You keep your mind busy, and your concentration levels are high, which enables you to keep your attention on the task that has to be completed.

An Appeal to Take Action

You should maintain a timer close by and make a note of the amount of time that you have committed to working. After you have worked for the allotted 25 minutes, you are entitled to a brief rest of five minutes. You are allowed to stop working and take a half-hour break once you have been doing so for about 2 hours.

In addition to this, schedule some time every day to engage in some kind of physical exercise. You may divide the total time you spend exercising each day into two parts: a morning session and an evening session.

There Are So Many Things To Do, But So Little Time.

Let's face it: life is made up of one work after another that has to be finished. You encounter it on a regular basis. The working mother who is rushing to send her kids to day care so that she can go to work on time. The high-powered corporate executive who is running late for his trip and yet hasn't bothered to pack his bags. A lot goes on in life. Having said that, the manner in which you conduct your company may have a significant impact on the amount of progress you make towards the goals you set for yourself in a single day.

You are not the only one who feels like there is never enough time in the day to get everything done that has to be done. A significant number of individuals are unable to successfully organise their time in order to complete their responsibilities in a timely manner. On the other hand, the thing that sets you apart from them is the fact that they aren't making any effort to modify their behaviour. For other people, they just accept the situation for what it is and go on nonetheless.

You were in the mood for something new when you started reading this book. You've observed that your day appears to fly by, and you're interested in putting yourself in a situation where there's a chance you'll be able to complete the tasks you've assigned to yourself while still having some spare time for other pursuits. You're already making progress towards altering that pattern of behaviour!

What I want you to take away from reading this book is the realisation that even if life is hectic, there is always time to work towards the goals you have set for yourself. It all comes down to how well you can organise your time. When I say this, what I mean is that this is the way in which you may fairly do the chores you face on a daily basis. You are not aiming to be a super hero by being in several locations at the same time. Therefore, let's get started with discovering methods to maximise your productivity by learning how to properly organise your day. One way to do this is to understand how to schedule your activities.

Take a Step Behind You

If you're anything like me, you have a tendency to rush headfirst into the day without giving it much thought beforehand. You are mentally running over a list of errands, and you are already plotting out the order in which you will do them. Nevertheless, it seems that there is always something that you forget. You went to the grocery store, but you failed to remind yourself that your kid needed something for a school assignment before you left.

When you first wake up, my recommendation is to pause for a moment, draw a full breath, and then take a few steps back from your racing thoughts. Take a piece of paper with you and jot down all of the tasks that need to be completed on that particular day. If it is in front of you, then you have a decent notion of the length of time that each one will take, and you can organise your style of attack more efficiently.

Make a Strategy

To guarantee that you are successful in completing the tasks on your to-do list, one of the simplest and most efficient things you can do is plan out your day. The vast majority of folks don't bother to complete this stage. It's almost as if they hit the button for the auto pilot, and then they simply charge forward.

Take some time to reflect on the order in which you do your tasks, and write down your thoughts. You may have a list that is long enough to wallpaper the bathroom, but if you plan it out and split it down, you will be able to do the activities that are the most essential to you first, before moving on to the chores that may not be as critical.

Hold fast to your strategy.

It is a very inefficient use of time to formulate a strategy with the intention of afterwards abandoning that strategy at the first chance that presents itself. When you do develop a strategy, you should try to adhere to it as best you can. Your day will not go precisely as you had intended for it to proceed because unexpected things will take place. The important thing is that you attempted to execute your strategy in the manner that you had envisioned it. Attend to the other matters as they present themselves.

Make Room for relaxation The notion of relaxation is foreign to those who are always on the go. People are willing to put their own requirements out of the way in order to fulfil the goals they have set for themselves. You should try to make it a priority to take a break at some point throughout the day. Depending on the specifics of your situation, this can include taking yourself out to lunch, seeing a buddy for coffee, or just picking up a book and reading a few chapters to relax and unwind. To prevent yourself from being completely exhausted by life, be sure to schedule in some time for relaxation.

Consider the following:

There are days when it is just not feasible to complete everything on your to-do list in the allotted 24 hours. There are certain days when everything that may go wrong does go wrong, and such days can consume your attention like nothing else could. Make sure that the activities that are the most essential to you are scheduled first as you plan out your day. Allow yourself the necessary amount of time to complete them. After you have finished, it would be wonderful if you could do other things if you still had time.

Everyone shares the sentiment that there should be more time in each day. However, knowing that this is not going to occur, we have no choice but to make do with the resources at our disposal. You will discover that if you learn how to be a good steward of your time and resources, you will be able to get into a pattern that will assist you in completing what you need to do in order to meet your obligations. Don't be that person who just follows everyone else's lead. That's OK on occasion, but in the long run it will result in unfinished business that cannot be avoided.

The Rule Of 21 Days To Overcome Your Tendency To Put Things Off

You have apparently completed the first step successfully. The second step, the third step, the fourth step, and the fifth step are all quite similar to the first step. You could even start to ponder about the advantages of doing these things on a regular basis and start to think about the value of doing these activities every day. Permit me to reassure you right now that the work that you are putting in is not in vain. You may not be able to notice the development since you are just starting off, but when a farmer puts seeds in the ground, do you expect to see a fully formed stalk of wheat the next day? One more time, there is no such thing as a quick route to achievement. Crawling is the necessary initial step for a youngster to take before they may learn how to walk. Building habits up to the point where it seems completely normal is exactly what we want to achieve.

The reason for this is because you have spent your whole life putting things off and putting them off. That is not a behaviour that can be changed in a single day. You need to devise a plan for the long run that will assist you in mitigating the adverse effects of the pattern of behaviour you've shown in the past.

Learn how to become a more self-disciplined person by following these steps:

The very first and most important issue that has to cross your thoughts is whether or not it is possible for you to improve as a person in only twenty-one days. The answer is unequivocally and unquestionably yes.

In only 21 days of your life, you have the potential to become a completely new person; nevertheless, you will need to continually keep working on improving your behaviours. You can't start doing something and then stop doing it later and expect to keep the benefits you've got from doing it in the first place. You have to realise that there is no end to the ways in which you may better yourself if you want to succeed in life, which is all about continual progress. If you go back to your old, unhealthy behaviours, you will, of course, lose out on any long-term advantages that could have been available to you. It's natural for individuals to go back to their previous behaviours every once in a while. This much is clear to everyone. It is tolerated as well as anticipated, but you are need to maintain regular attendance. Every every time you have a relapse, you need to get back on your feet and work on being a better version of yourself. There is no need in giving up; I think that you are trying to make changes in your life. If you have read up to this point, it is abundantly evident to me that you are aware that there is a problem, and that you want to find a solution to this problem.

You have made it through the stages of denial and fear, and there is no way that you should give up now that you have reached this point. It's possible that the road to success won't finish in 21 days, but if you follow this plan, it will pave a clear route and establish a strong foundation for you that you can continue to grow and build upon. If you work on improving your positive behaviours, you will become better over time and continue to evolve into a more admirable person.

Throughout the following 21 days, there are a few hints and suggestions that I will be sharing with you that will need careful execution on your part. These are tried-and-true strategies and recommendations that have assisted tens of thousands of individuals in developing greater self-control. If you follow their instructions to the letter, you will also benefit from them.

There is a limited amount of time available in this life, and each given day has the potential to be the person's last. It is important to keep in mind that the only way to be able to look back on your life without feeling regret is to spend it doing the things that you genuinely enjoy. In point of fact, it is preferable to die having spent one's life doing what one loves rather than passing away with one's reputation intact. You should never put your debts on the back burner, and you should always make sure that your financial existence is guaranteed. However, the reality is that after all has been said and done, the only thing that will remain is how you choose to spend your life.

The author of the book "The Top Five Regrets of the Dying," Bronnie Ware, was an extremely experienced nurse who wrote the book. Learning the things that individuals think about while they are lying in their last moments may be a defining moment in one's life. The following are the five most common things individuals say they regret after passing away.

I have always wished that I had the actual guts to go against what other people expected of me in life so that I could live a life that I truly liked and that was authentic to who I am.

This particular regret was believed to be the one that individuals pondered on the most often before they passed away out of everything else. When a person's life comes to a conclusion, they often think back on the many unrealized goals and ambitions they had throughout their lifetime. It was a very unusual occurrence for a person to be on their dying bed and have even half of their desires in life come true. The fact that they did not follow their aspirations while having the opportunity was the primary cause of their regret. "Health brings a freedom that very few people realise they have until it is taken away from them,"

I really regret that I wasted my whole life by working so hard.

When it comes to guys, this is an extremely regular occurrence. Due to the fact that they were always preoccupied with their profession, they were never able to participate in the upbringing of their children and they never had the chance to genuinely enjoy the company of their spouse. Even while keeping up with your financial obligations is of the utmost significance, there are instances when it is more beneficial to work more efficiently rather than harder. If you actually want to spend your whole life working, you should start making preparations for the bulk of it as soon as you realise that your available time has been depleted.

3. I really regret that I did not voice my emotions and stand up for my right to be treated as an individual.

This is just another demonstration of how significant time is. People are willing to give up their interests, affections, and aspirations in order to contribute to the establishment of a more tranquil atmosphere. People felt as if they never developed themselves into they genuinely thought they could be and spent their lives developing disease as a consequence of the bottled up bad feelings they carried within of them as a result of this regret. This is the reason why it is so necessary to reflect on this regret. People felt as though they never developed themselves into they truly believed they could be.

4. I really should have stayed in touch with my closest buddies.

Because of how hectic life can become, even the closest of friends might become estranged from one another for a variety of reasons, including distance and activity. It is quite simple to let a hectic lifestyle take control of your thoughts and allow even the most incredible friendships to fade away over the course of time. The fact that individuals regret not spending more time with their friends is among the top five things they wish they had done differently in their lives, which is a sad reality. Because your life without the people you care about can never be as big as the life you spend with your favourite people from all over the globe, it is essential to maintain social relationships and remain in contact with those you consider important.

I wish that I had allowed myself to have a happier life.

It shouldn't come as much of a shock that this item is included on the list. The importance of leading a joyful and loving life is something that a lot of people overlook. People usually come to the conclusion that happiness is a choice by the time they reach the end of their lives. People let their brains and their lives run amok because they are caught inside of their everyday lives, their environments, and the patterns of behaviour that they have developed through habit. The end effect was a life that was characterised by seriousness and feelings of dissatisfaction. Laughter, as well as bringing forth a person's pleasure, curiosity, and inner child, are some of the most valued reflections of individuals who are nearing the end of their lives.

The Real-World Application of Your Five-Year Vision:

There are seven phases involved in putting your five-year plan into action so that you may take charge of your life.

The first thing you need to do is compare and contrast the two ways in which you carry out each and every area of your day.

Keep in mind how you felt when you were having the best day ever.

Experience the feelings and precisely pinpoint the places in which you most enjoyed passing the time throughout a day bestowed by the gods. Keep a log of all of your time, just as you did in the previous chapter, and divide your activities into two distinct categories once again. The first group consists of your degrees of pleasure from one to three, two to six, and seven to ten. In order to get a deeper comprehension of life, the group is analysing how you use both your time at work and the time you have for yourself.

Now, contrast the day you are living with the day you dream of living, and get a sense of the difference that results from having control over time.

This distinct disparity in timing is referred to be your time forgetfulness.

Your temporal oblivion refers to the environmental and emotional disconnection that exists between the life you are living now and the one you want to live in five years.

Step 2: Make a list of the items in your life that can be improved right away by making very little adjustments.

While you are making comparisons between the day you are living and the day you are dreaming of living, it is very crucial to pinpoint the areas in which you can bridge the gap between your present life and the one you dream about living.

If you have a passion for viewing films, you may establish a media firm or a blog. This is just one example. If you have a passion for music, you should teach yourself how to play your chosen instrument. If you have a passion for a topic, consider turning that passion into a career as a teacher.

Whatever it is that you can do to fill your forgetfulness, it is imperative that you put direct action towards the things that you love. It is not uncommon for the things that you like doing the most in real life to mirror those that you enjoy doing in your dream day. Even if you don't have any links, that's still perfectly acceptable. Simply get rid of the elements of your five-year vision that aren't vital. Cutting out the things that aren't part of your goal will immediately provide place for you to achieve your 5 year vision. This may seem like a difficult task, but it's the reality.

If you have trouble finding the time to do things, see yourself as an elderly person and think that you are lying on your deathbed. Would you have any regrets if you continued living your life for the rest of your life precisely as it is right now? Would you be dissatisfied if you had to live out the rest of your life as today and the preceding thirty days, or would you wish you had seized this opportunity to live a life that you genuinely loved?

Step 3: Reverse-engineer your five-year objective all the way down to the present day, breaking it down into small weekly tasks from the beginning to the end, and tracking your progress as you go. Maintain meticulous documentation of the process of reverse engineering.

Take a look at the day of your dreams. Now suppose that you are winding down for the night and reflecting on the trip from your ideal day, but instead of beginning with that day, you start with the ideal day in your mind and play a movie in your brain of your journey all the way back in time to the day that you are living now.

It is going to seem overwhelming the first time you try to accomplish this, but it is a necessary step in the process of Taking Control of Time. Your dreams will never become a reality until you take action to create a connection between the day you dream about and the day you really live. I am a product of your creative thinking.

Be careful to write down everything that comes to mind when you go backwards in time from the day you spent dreaming, as you will want to remember everything you did. Now take a look at the significant milestones that you have completed and the time period in which you did so. This will make it much easier for you to have a solid understanding of how you will construct your schedule over the following few years and the route that will bring you straight to a life that you will really like living.

Strategy Formulation And Execution

A solid strategy for time management cannot exist without a solid action plan. Action plans are what you use to put your strategies and objectives into action. They are where you take your thoughts and make them into something tangible.

It is one thing to arrange your time in order to get things done, but before you can accomplish that, you need to have a clear understanding of the specific steps that need to be taken. This is beneficial to you in both your professional and personal life.

A solid action plan will guide you through the process of putting down what you want to do all the way up to the point when you actually accomplish it. If you are unable to put into action the steps necessary to complete the job that your employer wants you to perform, it is pointless for you to schedule out a sufficient amount of time to do so.

Dissecting the Action Plan into Its Individual Steps

There are a number of primary actions that may be broken down further for your action plan.

The first step is to classify the primary activities that must be completed in order to achieve all of the primary milestones.

Maintain a wide focus on these primary tasks. As an illustration of a person who is contemplating a change in career: Think about where you are now, where you want to be in the future, how you want to get there, what steps you will take to get there, and then review your progress.

Two, break down each large activity into many more manageable steps.

You are going to discover that you are required to go into greater information here. It is not required that you create a report that is 10 pages long, but it is guaranteed that you will need to undertake more research.

Third, think about if any of the primary responsibilities can be performed by someone else.

This phase is more appropriate for activities that are connected to business, but there need to be someone accepting complete responsibility for each work. Because of this, they will be aware of how far along the work they are, as well as what further has to be done and so on.

Identify any potentially significant problems that may develop, and make sure you have a backup plan.

This phase is sometimes referred to as "Risk Management," and its purpose is to identify potential issues and devise solutions for dealing with them in the event that they materialise.

As you can see, the implementation of action plans might take some time, which may seem odd given that you are attempting to determine methods that can assist you in properly managing your time. However, it is considerably more helpful to sacrifice some time at the beginning of a project or job in order to be able to go through it quickly all the way to completion than it is to continually stop and start working because you need to perform research for the next phase of the project.

Put an end to any and all unnecessary work.

Examine anything very carefully if you are currently working on something that has to be done. Do you really need to create a report that is twenty pages long and packed with diagrams and charts when a report that is 10 pages long and has two charts would be sufficient? Do you really need to send out an email with the instructions rather than calling a meeting with everyone to discuss what needs to be done when it would be easier and more effective to just send out an email?

When you get to the conclusion that it is not required to do everything, having a solid action plan might assist you in better managing your time. It is possible to hand over some responsibilities to other people, while others might be eliminated entirely. During the process of developing your action plan, you can discover that continuing to work on some aspects of the problem is a complete and utter waste of time and resources.

The first step is to prioritise the tasks.

Establishing a hierarchy for your responsibilities is the first step towards more efficient time management on your part. Do the things that are the most essential to you first, and reserve the chores that are the least important until the end. When you do this, you guarantee that the tasks that are the most essential are done on time. To do this, make a list of all of your responsibilities and prioritise them from most important to least important. After that, you may arrange them in descending order according to the amount of time required to finish each one. You should probably get started with the chores that need the greatest effort first, and then go on to the ones that are easy. Consider the significance of the activities. The activities that provide the greatest value to your company should be completed first, while the duties that contribute the least value should be completed last of all. The key to success in this endeavour is to ensure that you finish all of your vital and urgent work first. Any time is suitable for doing things that are routine. Putting your tasks in order of importance helps you choose the sequence in which you should do them. Because priorities might shift at any moment, you need to be adaptable. It's possible that you won't be able to complete all of the tasks. You have the option of omitting the ones that may not be relevant.

The second step is to not take on more than you are capable of managing.

You should never take on more responsibility than you are capable of managing. Never be frightened to reject an offer. Your life will likely get disrupted because you are unable to say "no," and as a result, you will take on more responsibilities than you are capable of completing. In order to be able to properly manage your time, it is essential to be aware of your limits and to be able to decline engagement in activities that are not of critical significance. Make sure that you are capable of completing the assignments you accept, and don't throw away your time on things that you won't be able to do. Saying "no" to requests until you have the time to complete them is the best course of action if you already have too much to accomplish. It is to one's detriment to take on too many responsibilities, despite the fact that taking on commitments in general is a positive thing to do. Be aware of what you are capable of and what you are unable to do at any given moment. It won't harm to just come out and say "No, I do not have time for this." It would hurt worse to agree to do the task, only to find out that you ran out of time before you could do it. This stage is all about not being scared to say no when you need to, as well as saying no when you need to.

Step 3: Ensure You Get Enough Rest

Your ability to effectively manage your time will benefit greatly by getting an adequate amount of sleep. Every night, you should aim to obtain between seven and eight hours of sleep at the absolute least. You could believe that if you slept for less hours each night, you would have more time to devote to your responsibilities. This is a serious error. If you were exhausted, you would probably be less productive than if you were well rested. When you go about your business, being alert and not too fatigued will be much easier for you if you have had a sufficient amount of sleep the night before. Maintain a consistent sleep schedule by going to bed and waking up at the same time each night and morning. Every night I go into bed around ten o'clock, and I wake up at six o'clock in the morning. Your ability to effectively manage your time will improve if you stick to a routine. Do not fall into the trap of believing that you will be able to increase your level of productivity by working when you should be resting rather than sleeping. If you follow the advice given in this stage, you will find that your mind is clearer and that you have improved cognitive abilities. I just cannot stress this point enough. People who obtain the recommended amount of sleep each night are statistically shown to have higher levels of productivity than those who do not. Make sure that you have had enough rest.

The fourth step is to get rid of any distractions.

It is so simple to get sidetracked and unable to focus on the work at hand. Prepare a place where you won't be disturbed while you work so you can give your whole attention to the activities at hand. The ideal situation is to have a home office in which you can work. Put away your phone, turn off the television, and so forth. It's okay to put on some tunes if it helps you focus, but you should minimise any other potential distractions as much as possible. It is recommended that you shut all of the windows on your internet browser. In my opinion, the home office should be a separate, private area, and you should instruct your family not to disturb you when you are working unless it is an absolute need. It is best to put your phone on vibrate and hide it from sight if you want to avoid being distracted by it, despite how tempting it may be to keep your phone nearby. If you want to be able to give your whole attention to the work at hand, you have to be able to separate yourself from the things that distract you on a regular basis. If you can only remember these instructions, you will be successful. You should be able to concentrate on the work at hand, and making sure that you adhere to the rules that are provided in this phase will assist you in being able to do so.

The Study Of Patterns That Lead To Achievement

Everyone is a victim to the power of their own habits. There are healthy habits, unhealthy habits, neutral habits, and so on.

When you want to become more productive and learn how to successfully manage your time, it is vital to thoroughly review all of your habits and determine which ones are assisting you in achieving your objectives and which ones are hindering your development or just wasting valuable time.

In addition to this, you need to acquire the ability to transform significant responsibilities, namely those that you want to do on a daily basis, into habits.

In this chapter, we are going to discuss the science behind habit triggers and habit loops, as well as how to establish new habits, how to evaluate and fix your existing habits, and how to form new habits.

When it comes to being skilled in the art of time management, all of this information is necessary knowledge.

Make use of cues to establish useful patterns of behaviour.

Let's say you want to become more effective in your current role. In order to accomplish this goal, you will most likely need to form the habit of doing additional work at home, conducting research, reading various books or articles, and so on.

On the other hand, the temptation to just give in to sloth and...just not do anything is always there. To have to go out and engage in all of that effort and develop those positive routines seems to be a chore that is quite laborious and wearisome.

To assist you in your endeavour, triggers are available.

What exactly is a trigger, then?

Mary Lamia, Ph.D., a clinical psychologist, believes that when an emotion is activated in your brain, your neurological system reacts by producing this subtle sensation in your body that is commonly referred to as a gut feeling, which impacts your choices.

The words of other people, the content of anything you see on television, the food you consume, or any one of a variety of other mundane, daily activities might set off an emotional reaction in you.

I would want for you, just for today, to pay extra close attention to how you are feeling. Take note of the little things—be they sights, sounds, or words—that may shift your mood significantly.

Make a mental or physical note of any specific acts that, when you do them, make you feel driven, excited, or eager. If you identify any particular behaviours that do this, do so.

This may be anything as simple as smiling at a member of your family, cuddling with your beloved pet cat, or simply cleaning your teeth first thing in the morning.

Make a note of whatever it is that gives you even a trace of excitement, even if it's just a little bit.

In addition to that, make it a point to be aware of the factors that contribute to your feelings of lethargy, depression, sloth, or lack of motivation. These are the triggers that you want to steer clear of entirely, or at the very least minimise your exposure to as much as you can.

Let's imagine there's this one individual — maybe a casual acquaintance — who you get in touch with every once in a while. Having a conversation with that someone, on the other hand, causes you to lose part of your drive and enthusiasm to get things done, and this happens each time you have a conversation with them. This might be because of anything that they say to you with the aim of causing you pain, or it could be because of something that they are completely unaware of. In any case, it is in your best interest to limit the amount of time you spend interacting with this particular individual. It may sound harsh, particularly if they are not doing it on purpose; nonetheless, there are occasions when you need to put yourself first, and this is one of those situations. You need to put yourself first in this situation.

Get rid of whomever or whatever it is that is having an emotional impact on you in a manner that is preventing you from getting things done by removing it from your life.

After you have accomplished this, you will be able to start concentrating on the positive triggers. Include in your daily routine activities that are able to elicit a favourable emotional response from you. Afterwards, immediately follow the positive trigger with the habit that is expected of you in order to make progress towards your objective.

If you do this every single day, you will eventually learn to identify the trigger with the habit, and it won't be nearly as difficult for you to stop being lazy and stop procrastinating because of the pleasurable sensation you get from doing it.

Now that we've covered triggers, let's speak about habit loops, which are also connected to triggers but include distinct sorts of triggers.

14 Time that has Already Gone Away Cannot Be Retrieved

I have misappropriated my time, and now time is consuming my life.

— William Shakespeare

This is the first thing that has to be determined: whether or not we are carrying out the task in accordance with the plan. Check it again in the middle and make adjustments if required. As a direct consequence of this, tasks may be completed quickly. New ideas are continually in a state of novelty. Therefore, there is no need for it. When you attempt new things or perceive old ones in a new light, you can end yourself wasting a lot of time and missing the deadline entirely. It is important to keep in mind that the combination of two ideas is the mother of creativity.

The Cost of a Split Second

Time is without a doubt the most valuable commodity there is in our planet. Time is the resource that we squander the most. This is due to the fact that we are unable to comprehend the significance of time until it has already gone.

During the process of maturing from a kid into a young adult, we devote time to learning. In exchange, we shall get some characteristics back. Because you put less hours into education, we have had to spend a greater portion of our remaining lifespan on it. Therefore, in those situations in which we will need to spend less time in the long run, you will need to spend more time in the short run. If you show stinginess in such situation, you will have to make up for it for the rest of your life. Spend the majority of your time, regardless of the field in which you work, initially on gaining an understanding of how things are done. There is no need to act like a miser over there. If you control the flow of time, you have the power to command the whole planet. This will not change in any way as time passes. Every time you have shown care for someone, that person will always show concern for you in return.

The Significance of Time

Time management and effective use of the time you have are vital components of a successful approach to any aspect of life. If one disregards the passage of time, it is impossible for them to achieve achievement. Everyone in the world who has ever taken the steps necessary to achieve success is a great man because they understand the magnificence of time. It will take one second to bind success, and it will take one second to bind failure.

The value of money is used to compare the passage of time. When people have invested part of their money, then they will be more responsible with how they utilise their money. After then, and only then, will they be able to use those funds for a variety of objectives in the future. To ensure a prosperous future, we must also spend our time.

If time management is a lovely skill, then understanding how others spend their own time is something that we are familiar with. The most common cause of wasted time is operating without a clear plan of action or a prioritised list of tasks. Making an effort to multitask might be exhausting. Keeping themselves occupied by fielding unwelcome phone calls. Trying to avoid doing the task and breaking the habit of consistently saying "no."

Time is the locomotive that drives the trip we call life. Because of this, we need to be aware of both what to do and what not to do. It is important to be aware of one's own skills and energy circle. By doing the necessary exercises, you may eventually become the master of time. Always keep your end objective in mind and arrange your to-do list in descending order of importance. Organise a method in advance so that the task may be finished quickly and simply. The task that you begin first is the work that you should finish first. Make sure you set aside some time to work on improving your skills. Keep a writing pad with you at all times so that you may jot down notes on significant events or works. Don't always respond with a "yes." Describe the job that has been finished. Always make sure the study space is spotless. Take some time for yourself to get things in order so that you can address the problems that are occurring in your immediate environment.

The key to achieving success on both an individual and a societal level is to revere time, or, more precisely, to make effective use of one's available time. Your life will take on a luminous quality if you treat each passing moment as if it were a candle. We are readily able to distinguish between any two works. There is absolutely no room for doubt.

The Artharva Veda gives a representation of time in the shape of a horse. Time passes quickly just as quickly as the horse rides quickly. In the same way that the sun shines brightly in seven different hues, time brings more light into the whole globe. Everyone in the world is aware of the power of the sun in the same way that they are aware of the magnitude of time. Time will be youthful, full of vitality, and everlasting. Time will never get stale. There is no task in the world that is not constrained by time. Everything else in the universe, with the exception of the Soul, God, and nature, will be at the mercy of time. Every other kind of life is on an equal footing with time. It does nothing except wait for a window of opportunity. Those individuals who have reached their maximum age will perish as a result.

There will be no opportunity to engage in any kind of labour once this body reaches old age and is unable to perform any function. Then they would walk away from their jobs, their houses, and everything else. Time will continue to pass regardless of whether or not the rest of the world is awake. The significance and magnitude of time's influence cannot be overstated. It is possible to regain any lost resources, such as money, a kingdom, one's health, or knowledge. The time that has already been lost can never be recovered.

The Benefits And Drawbacks Of Multitasking When Managing Your Time

The practise of being able to accomplish numerous tasks at the same time is referred to as multitasking. You could, for instance, make changes to a paper while both responding to an email and participating in a teleconference at the same time.

During the interview process, most companies will inquire of prospective workers about their level of proficiency in multitasking. The vast majority of businesses are looking for workers who can multitask well without, of course, sacrificing the quality of their output.

It's important to remember that multitasking is a delicate phenomena that, if not managed properly, might result in spending more time than is necessary on the activities at hand. Should you fully avoid multitasking in order to get things done more quickly, or should you try to multitask in order to get things done faster? This chapter will discuss the different advantages and drawbacks of multitasking, as well as provide you with some fundamental pointers, and show you how to make the most of its potential in a variety of settings.

The Value of Being Able to Multitask

When it comes to juggling many responsibilities at once, there are a few benefits that just must not be neglected. Let us take a look at some of these advantages and the contexts in which they function well.

Multitasking makes it possible to do simple, everyday chores in a time efficient manner – Here are several situations in which it is more productive to switch between many tasks at once rather than concentrating on just one of them in order to get things done more quickly.

It is possible for a parent to prepare breakfast, pack the lunch box for their kid, eat breakfast, and converse on the phone all at the same time, and it is probable that all of these tasks will be completed well.

In a similar vein, if you are working on a specific task when you are at your place of employment, it is feasible to do other things, such as listen to music or react to a basic email enquiry, with little to no impact on your financial situation.

The second example can still be a reason for worry when it comes to achieving the level of quality that is necessary. On the other hand, if you are an experienced expert, it is feasible to get results that are of an uncompromisingly high quality.

Building your resistance to distractions may be facilitated by practising multitasking. The contemporary, tech-savvy world is full with countless distractions that come in a variety of forms, such as updates on social networking platforms, the most recent newsfeeds, urgent answers to emails, YouTube videos on a variety of topics related to the globe, and many more. This state of affairs, in which all of these diversions compete with one another to get our attention, will continue forever.

Building up your resistance to these never-ending distractions might be aided by practising multitasking. Because our mind is so full with, and also distracted by, the several jobs that need to be accomplished concurrently, it is easy able to fight the powerful pull of the kinds of distractions that are not productive. You will notice that it is simple to place a mental reminder to come back later and check on that social media update that was very fascinating of a close buddy, a gossip item alert about your favourite star, or anything else of the kind.

The ability to multitask allows you to make progress on numerous things at the same time . When you multitask, it is feasible to make slow but steady progress on all of the activities that you are working on at the same time. There are many instances in which the due dates for several projects coincide with one another; yet, it is essential that all of the projects be filed in the right manner. When faced with challenges of this kind, the ability to multitask is of critical importance. You may choose to collaborate on two or three different projects. The following are some examples of typical situations. Today, before 4 o'clock, you are responsible for delivering a presentation as well as submitting a report that you have been assigned to complete.

Let's say that each of these endeavours need inputs from a variety of different places. You may finish the part of the work that is tied to the data that you have received as and when you get these inputs for one of the tasks. You will probably have received specific inputs for the other assignment by the time you get to that point. After that, you may switch to it and complete the tasks that need to be done. In this way, you will be able to work on each of the tasks as soon as you get necessary data, and you will also be able to move between the tasks according to your preferences and the importance of the jobs.

Taking this strategy will assist you in finishing both of your tasks on time and without sacrificing the quality of your work. In order to maintain a high level of quality when multitasking, it is essential that you pay careful attention to each individual step of the process.

You may bring some semblance of order to an otherwise chaotic environment by practising multitasking. At your place of employment, particularly in this age of advanced technology, you get instructions from a number of different sources all at once. Unlike in previous times, when instructions were provided orally either via morning meetings or directly from bosses sitting a few cubicles away from your job, instruction messages now arrive through email, internal office communication channels, text messages, and more. In former times, instructions were given verbally either through morning meetings or directly from bosses sitting a few cubicles away from your workplace.

It's possible that your employer is really stationed in a whole other part of the world. In addition, it's possible that other members of your team may come to you for assistance. In addition, almost everything has to be completed 'immediately.' In a world where distractions are so widespread that you cannot avoid them at any cost, multitasking may assist bring some semblance of order to the chaos that exists there.

Quickly Adapt To Any Changes

As someone who has a background in engineering, I have seen several examples like this during the course of my career. You get started on a project, but then the conditions shift, and you find yourself with an outcome that is utterly unrelated to what you had envisioned. The outcome may or may not be in line with your expectations, but regardless, it is the product of reality, and in the end, there are times when there is no other choice than to go along with it.

If there is an issue that cannot be addressed or cannot be solved in the manner that you want to solve it, you should get yourself ready to shift your viewpoint and swiftly adapt to a new strategy. If you don't, you'll end up wasting a lot of time by sticking with what you believe to be the one and only right approach to carry out certain tasks.

You may quickly adjust to changes in a number of ways, all of which will keep you from feeling too horrible about the situation:

Evaluation of trust: Do not undertake activities without first measuring their effects or creating some kind of record of their progress. If you do that, you are engaging in guesswork, and it will be difficult to comprehend issues, generate answers, identify viable improvements, and come to intelligent conclusions. If you have the data, you can use analytical tools to accomplish any one of these goals. Obtaining the data could seem to be a pointless use of your time, yet it is very essential. People that work with you or for you at your place of employment will say things like "That is occurring because this, this, and this." They might be correct or they could be wrong. They may even have highly persuasive arguments that are not founded on facts that can be independently verified. However, in the absence of evidence, there is essentially no way of knowing what is taking place. Engineers make it a point to prove whatever they can, and they often do research on matters that they may not even need to present to their supervisor. Despite the fact that the issue has been resolved or the solution has been made, the company continues to save the data so that it may use it as a reference in the future.

I am aware that it is not always possible to stop what you are doing in a fast-paced work environment in order to gather data and offer measurable evidence to everything. It is often necessary to find solutions to issues as rapidly as is humanly feasible. However, precision should be a factor in every problem-solving scenario you encounter. Although finding a solution to it may take more time right now, it may mean that you will never have to face that challenge again in the future. Finding a solution that is feasible over the long term today, rather than waiting finding a solution for making little tweaks that need to be performed regularly, can save you time in the long run and help you save more time overall. To put it another way, you can sew as many patches onto your worn-out trousers as you like, but at some point you will need to replace them with brand-new ones. Instead of having to purchase a new pair of trousers, you will be able to mend the ones that are damaged via analysis. On the other hand, it can just advise you to get a new one. Analysis, however, will help you save time regardless of what it reveals to you since it will show you what is incorrect and what can be done to correct it.

Let's assume for the sake of argument that there are two persons in this scenario. One individual is an excellent communicator and can convince others to believe whatever they want them to believe. And a second individual has reliable measurements and analysis that point in the opposite direction of what the first individual is claiming. Pay attention to what the first person is saying, but if the evidence shows anything that runs counter to what the first person is arguing, you need to believe the analysis. In the event if both the evidence and the views go in the same direction, you do not have to be concerned about who to trust and may instead proceed with the proper action.

This illustrates the fundamental distinction between facts and views. Believing in facts takes priority over believing in views if you will be deciding on a course of action, attempting to solve an issue, or implementing changes. Why? Simply because it reduces the amount of time needed. If there isn't any data or analysis, those in charge of making decisions will have to rely on speculation to guide their actions. This process will be repeated over and over again without end, wasting everyone's time in the process. It's a little like riding on a carousel. A youngster may walk in circles for a considerable distance, but in the end, the child will have made no forward progress at all.

Learn to identify and address the problem's underlying causes: What factors contributed to the development of the problem? This is a fundamental principle used in engineering. If you are able to determine the underlying cause of a problem whenever one arises, you will have immediately saved a significant amount of time that would have otherwise been spent attempting to fix things that do not matter or even changing things that have nothing to do with the real issue, which would have made things worse and caused extra time to be wasted. This is particularly the case when something was functioning well in the past but all of a sudden began to give people trouble. It's possible that the underlying problem is something as simple as new workers who have been given training but are failing to assemble products in accordance with the right production processes. It's possible that someone on the manufacturing floor felt they had discovered a superior technique for assembly, and their coworkers began putting the product together in this manner because they believed it was 'easier' or 'more practical' to do so. It's possible that the issue is caused by something external, such a change in the specifications for a product that was created by a supplier. In situations like these, the issue may be remedied by communicating with the individuals in charge of assembly or contacting the supplier.

The bottom line is that if something has been operating well and then all of a sudden you start having issues with it, you need to realise that something has changed and work as quickly and correctly as you can to figure out what the problem is. It is always vital to keep records of critical procedures since, in the absence of such data, it is very difficult and time consuming to determine the underlying cause of any issue.

When you have identified the fundamental problem, resolving it promptly will, in most instances, be the most time- and labor-effective course of action. It might be as simple as a five-minute discussion with your business partners, staff, or even your superior.

Consult with, or at least take into consideration the recommendations of, experts: Sometimes, the underlying problem may not be an easy one to solve, and even if the persons involved have the necessary knowledge or information at their disposal, it may still be impractical to arrive at a decision. You could discover that a problem is having a negative impact on the company, and that by making some very little adjustments, the issues seem to be momentarily resolved, but they keep resurfacing again and again. At this point, it is possible that you may need assistance from a third party. Call the servicing department of the company providing the goods or services your company uses and ask them to send an expert. This is especially important to do if the products or services come from a third party. On occasion, issues may be resolved during the course of a conversation through e-mail or the telephone, but at other times, it may be necessary for someone to come over and have a look at what is taking place. It is possible that this will save the company a significant amount of time since professionals have spent a significant amount of time perfecting their craft, and it is very probable that they will spot the problem much more quickly. If you do this, there is a possibility that you will incur some charges; nevertheless, this is preferable than squandering all of that time and man hours, which, in the long run, will cost more than just bringing in an expert.

The Management Of Time And Its Tools

There are a variety of tools at your disposal that you may use to efficiently manage your time. We are going to focus on the most significant aspects of them in the next chapter.

I. Records of Past Events

Writing down how you spend your time is the primary purpose of keeping an activity log, which is also often called a work activity log or an activity diary. By keeping a journal of your actions for many days in a row, you may get an accurate picture of how you invest and use your time throughout the course of the day. Instead of depending on your memory, which may be a poor guide, you should keep a journal of your activities. You will discover that the experience to be rather eye-opening and informative.

You will be able to decide, with the assistance of your activity record, whether or not the job that is most important to you is completed at the appropriate time of the day. As an example, you could feel more inspired and full of energy in the morning, which indicates that the most important job you have to perform should be completed at this time of the day. After that, you are free to devote the rest of the day to focusing on less critical chores, such as returning phone calls or replying to emails, as these activities demand less effort.

You may also identify non-core tasks or activities, which are those that take up a significant amount of your time but do not directly contribute to the achievement of your important goals. For instance, you could discover that the afternoon routine entails a significant amount of time spent either brewing coffee or perusing the internet. Now that you have this information, you can modify your activity log so that it only includes the most relevant actions and deletes the activities that are a waste of your time.

A. Instructions for Establishing an Activity Record

You can simply obtain free activity journal templates here, or you may use a spreadsheet to construct one from start. Both options are readily available. After creating a new spreadsheet document in a spreadsheet programme such as Microsoft Excel, put the following items as the column headings for the activity log that you are going to set up:

The time and date

Description of the Activity Feelings (or how you are now feeling) in relation to the Activity

Time Spent on an Activity

Value of the Activity; this might be high, low, medium, or even none at all.

In addition to that, be sure to document all of your job tasks as they are completed.

You need to keep a log of everything you do, how you feel at that particular time (flat, energetic, alert, tired, etc.), and the time the change occurs, whenever you change activities (for example, making coffee, responding to an email, talking to coworkers, or even working on a report, etc.). This will help you understand how your body reacts to different activities and how you can better manage it.

You will be able to go back over your activity record at a later time and analyse it, taking into account the part that each action played in bringing you closer to achieving your objectives. You will be able to note the amount of time spent on each activity, as well as whether the activity was of low, medium, or high value.

B. Learning from the Activity Log

After you have used the diary to record your activities for a few days, you will need to assess its usefulness. You may be shocked to learn how much of your time you spend on activities that have little to no value. You will be able to discern the times of the day when you are energetic and the periods of the day when you are not energetic based on the pauses you take to relax, your natural disposition, food, and even the kind of job that you perform.

After reviewing your activity record, increase your output by engaging in the following productive endeavours to further your progress:

Tasks that will not help you achieve your goals and objectives should either be delegated to someone else or eliminated entirely. This is also true for tasks that are not a part of your responsibilities and that may thus be completed by another individual.

Plan to do the activities that you believe to be the most hard at the periods of the day when you have the most energy. This will guarantee that you not only do such duties in a shorter amount of time, but also that the work you generate is of a higher quality.

Reduce the amount of times that you are allowed to transition between different types of tasks. For instance, you may make it such that certain categories of tasks are worked on once a day or many times a week, depending on your preference.

Make it a priority to limit the amount of time you spend on things like preparing coffee and other personal tasks. This is a job that can be done as a group by taking turns, which will save time and enhance the team's morale at the same time.

You Should Prioritise The Management Of Your Energy Rather Than Your Time.

Take charge of your power use.

Techniques for managing your energy should be your starting point if you want to be able to effectively manage your time. Many manuals on time management approach the resource "Time" as if it were eternally administrable. As though by properly organising your day, you would be able to make the most of the time you have available and accomplish more than you ever have before. But the reality is that time management is not quite as easy as it may seem.

If your body does not have enough energy throughout the day to keep up with a systematically planned time management strategy, you are not going to be effective at work. Planning and scheduling are crucial, but it is even more important that you address your energy levels before trying to corral your hectic working hours into a time management system. This should be done before you try to plan and schedule.

The following is a discussion on three extremely important aspects of your life that should help you get a better understanding of how the amounts of energy you have effect your total productivity.

Your Prescribed Bedtime Routine

Your capacity to get a good night's sleep, feel relaxed and rejuvenated when you get up early in the morning, and be ready to get started on a productive day is directly correlated to the quality of sleep you get. Hormones that are created in the body naturally, such as dopamine and adrenaline, are responsible for regulating your attention and keeping you focused on the task at hand. The synthesis of these hormones is decreased, which in turn leads to a decrease in one's level of productivity while at work.

This may be caused by chronic sleep problems or regular short periods of sleep.

A number of studies have shown that getting an adequate quantity of sleep each night helps individuals improve their ability to recall and absorb new knowledge, as well as their resilience and creativity when they are at work. Memory is enhanced, and one's ability to perform better on intellectually hard activities, such as competing on examinations and handling tough job deadlines, may be improved by getting better quality sleep.

Suggestions for more restful sleeping

Keep a consistent hour for going to bed: Establish a regular hour for going to bed, and stick to it even on the weekends. You should try to get into the habit of going to bed at the exact same hour every night, regardless of whether or not you feel fatigued. If you need to modify when you go to bed, try making adjustments that aren't too drastic, such going to bed 10 or 20 minutes earlier or later.

Get out of bed at the same time every day: If you go to bed at a reasonable hour and stay asleep for around seven to eight hours, you should be able to get up at the same time every day without the need for an alarm. If you find that you have to set an alarm in order to get up in the morning, this almost certainly indicates that you aren't getting enough sleep at night.

Nap during the middle of the day: If you find that you are not able to get enough sleep at night, you might consider taking a nap during the day to make up for the lost sleep rather than deviating from your typical sleep schedule. If you have trouble sleeping, you should avoid napping.

It's normal to feel drowsy after supper on certain days, but you shouldn't go to bed earlier than you normally would. Stay away from the bedroom and engage in some activity that will provide you with a moderate amount of stimulation, such as going for a stroll or doing the dishes.

Before going to bed, make sure your computer and television are turned off, and avoid playing games that are too stimulating or watching TV episodes that are too violent. The process of falling asleep is slowed down by these stimulating activities. Instead of doing that, try listening to some soothing music or reading a book.

If you want to read, get an e-reader instead of using a gadget with a backlight like an iPad.

Maintain a dark and cold temperature in your bedroom, preferably about 18 degrees Celsius.

Make sure you are sleeping on a comfy bed or mattress.

Things that you need to stay away from before going to bed

It is not a good idea to have a hearty meal just before going to bed. This will prevent digestion and leave you feeling nauseous after you've finished eating.

Avoid consuming alcohol in the hours leading up to bedtime. Consuming alcohol in the hours before night causes sleep to be less restful.

Before going to bed, stay away from coffee and cigarettes, and don't use any sleeping drugs.

What You Should Eat to Have a Productive Day

The foods you consume have a significant impact on the amount of energy you have. Every person is different, which means that the ways in which they approach their nutrition are also unique. Consuming meals that are highly processed and based on simple carbohydrates on a regular basis deprives your body of the vitamins, minerals, and nutrients it needs to function at its optimal level. Your mental capacity will increase, and you will remain focused and productive throughout the day if you eat in a way that is both balanced and healthful. The majority of the nutrients in the food you eat are converted into glucose by your body. Glucose is the primary fuel that keeps your body and brain functioning properly. You may keep your body active all day long by eating certain nutritious meals, such as complex carbohydrates, which release glucose into the bloodstream in a slow and steady manner. Consume foods that are made from whole grains. Here are a few pointers to help you better regulate your energy levels.

Breakfast should never be skipped: Breakfast should not be skipped, and it should be a nutritious meal consumed each morning. Consuming a nutritious breakfast can assist you in remaining active throughout the day. Include complex carbohydrates, such as bread and cereals made with whole grains.

Consume a number of modest meals throughout the day. Consume a series of meals that are relatively modest but more often spaced apart. This way of eating can help you maintain a healthy blood pressure and provide you the energy you need to be productive throughout the day. Keep in mind that moderation is essential, which means that you should end a meal feeling content rather than full.

Consume plenty of water and meals that are high in fibre. Just like foods that are high in complex carbohydrates, foods that are high in fibre digest slowly and keep your body active. Consume a diet that is high in fibre, and aim to drink at least eight glasses of water every day.

Caffeine and alcohol: During the day, you should limit yourself to drinking just the right quantity of coffee. Coffee should be consumed out of a cup made of green tea. The common belief is that having a big cup of coffee first thing in the morning will help keep you energetic throughout the day, but drinking too much coffee might cause a crash that reduces your productivity. Because it will make it difficult for you to go to sleep, avoid consuming alcohol after supper and in the hours leading up to bedtime.

Foods that might make or break your productivity for the day

Salmon: Salmon, particularly wild salmon, is an excellent source of omega-3 fatty acids, vitamin B, and iron. Consuming salmon regularly may assist enhance brain function and maintain mental concentration.

Berries: Berries contain a significant amount of antioxidants. Memory is improved, and both mental and physical coordination are improved as a result of their use.

Vitamin B may be found in abundance in organic eggs. Memory is one of the areas that may be helped by vitamin B, which also helps to speed up the body's response time.

Eggplant: Studies have shown that eating eggplant may aid increase communication impulses between brain cells and the messenger chemicals that are present in the brain.

Green Tea: Green tea is loaded with health-benefiting antioxidants. Drinking green tea provides your body with a neuroprotective benefit and helps the neurological system perform at a higher level for longer.

Consume enough of dark leafy greens to help you get more done during the day. Iron, minerals, and phytonutrients may all be found in dark green leafy vegetables. Your brain cells get more oxygen thanks to the iron in the dark leafy greens, which also helps increase your cognitive control over those brain cells.

Milk chocolate has been shown to increase both visual and verbal memory, as well as the ability to respond more quickly. Dark chocolate, on the other hand, is known to boost attention and concentration.

Foods high in calcium Calcium, which may be obtained via diet, ensures that your nervous system remains in peak operating condition. High-quality calcium may be found in foods like milk and cheese, as well as in green vegetables and beans.

Yoghurt: probiotics, proteins, and minerals may all be found in yoghurt with a reduced amount of fat. Yoghurt is beneficial to your digestive system, and studies suggest that the probiotics included in yoghurt make you more likely to live a longer life.

Products eaten that have a negative impact on work efficiency

Consuming meals and beverages that are high in sugar might lead to feelings of confusion, nervousness, and weakness.

Consuming high-calorie items like hamburgers and fries can impair your performance at work and cause you to feel tired. After that, you drink even more coffee, which just makes the situation worse.

Consuming an insufficient amount of food might be detrimental to your productivity. This will make it difficult for you to recall information and will also slow down your reaction time.

Regular Workouts and a Productive Lifestyle

Exercising not only makes you healthier physically but also more productively mentally and emotionally. Exercising gives you more energy, improves your mood, and makes you smarter. The following are some of the advantages of regular exercise:

Exercising not only gives your body the energy it needs but also makes you more alert: Physical activity increases the amount of blood that flows to the brain, helping you to remain alert and ready to face difficult challenges at work. The additional energy you get from exercise allows you to complete your tasks more swiftly.

Generally makes things easier to deal with: Regular exercise not only makes you healthier but also provides you the energy to deal with the strenuous physical demands of your job. If your body is healthy and strong, you will have a lower risk of being hurt on the job.

Enhances both physical and mental health: According to a number of studies, physical activity is beneficial to mental health and may reduce feelings of worry and sadness. Serotonin, sometimes known as the "feel-good" hormone, is produced in greater quantities when one engages in physical activity. Your mood may be helped by serotonin, which also makes you feel better overall. You have realised that when you are not overwhelmed by stress and are in a good mood, you are able to do difficult activities more quickly.

Assists in warding off illness Regular exercise that engages the whole body, such as brisk walking, jogging, or swimming, may assist in warding off illness and other health issues, including obesity, hypertension, coronary heart disease, and type 2 diabetes.

Include physical activity in your daily routine.

When mowing the grass, quicken your pace.

Instead of driving, you could walk your children to school and run back home.

When you have the opportunity, go swimming.

While you're watching television, try doing some simple exercises.

Get your housekeeping done as fast as possible.

Regularly take the dog for a walk.

Quicken your pace as you make your way to the bus stop or train station.

Perform some physical activity on your lunch break.

Do some exercise with your next-door neighbour.

Engage in activities that you enjoy:

An enjoyable pastime that one enjoys, such as dance, cycling, or horseback riding

Engage in some physical activity, such as tennis, baseball, basketball, or bowling.

You may become more productive with only a few days' worth of little adjustments.

Putting Too Many Goals In Front Of You Might Be Distracting.

When I worked with this person, they were always trying to satisfy everyone, but in the end, they satisfied nobody. The unfortunate reality is that it is impossible to please everyone all of the time. What you can do is pick what should be given the most importance. When it was brought to this woman's attention that she was squandering her time and being less productive than others, she became quite unhappy. However, once she gained an understanding of how to prioritise her tasks, she was able to do a much greater amount of work. You have to choose what the most important thing is that has to be done today and get it done. You shouldn't allow other things stand in the way of your progress. She was devoting an inordinate amount of her time to attending to the needs of clients who did not play a significant role in the operation of the business. "How am I supposed to ignore them?

She was right when she said, "They are customers," but these were customers who were spending so little that eating into that amount of her time, she was neglecting customers who were actually frustrated by not being able to contact staff when they needed to and who were first-rate customers bringing in sufficient profit to pay her wages. She was ignoring customers who were upset because they could not contact staff when they needed to.

So, how do you deal with the other people that are calling?

If you have a screening service or a secretary, make sure that they are aware of the company's policies about the calls that you accept, and direct them to ensure that low-priority callers are not let through. If you answer your own calls, make sure that every call goes to voicemail so that you may sort them in the order that is most important to you. It is not worth your time to answer each of these calls since doing so will prevent you from reaching the goal you have set for yourself.

There is however another method that may be used to route calls, and if you have ever attempted to contact your bank, you have most likely come across this method at some point. A piece of software is used to filter incoming calls in such a way that callers are sent to various buttons if they want to speak to a different department.

You are able to carry out the same action. Recognise patterns so that when someone calls you on a regular basis and you need to transfer that call to someone else – they receive a message reminding them that if they require............ service, then they need to redial and ask for extension... a, thereby relieving the weight off of your telephone. This can be done so that when someone calls you on a regular basis and you need to transfer that call to someone else. By leaving a message stating that customers should contact you via the business website rather than by phone, you might encourage individuals to do so. The individual who called will not be as annoyed if they are simply informed that you are unable to take their call.

Eliminating the use of the mobile phone

Mobile phones are yet another hindrance to productivity. Yes, of course they serve a role, and in this day and age, it is quite unlikely that anybody would expect you to operate without one. On the other hand, they turn out to be one of the most distracting things that can be found. Imagine this: you are in the midst of a difficult set of mathematical calculations at work, attempting to determine the viability of an idea that you want to offer to your coworkers. You should care about it since it may lead to a promotion. The phone starts to ring. Your wife would really appreciate it if you could pick up the dry cleaning after the day is through. After that, you jot down a reminder to carry out the aforementioned action. You set it down, and just as you do so, you become aware of a new status post on your Facebook account, which causes you to question what is going on. In addition to that, you have three emails from folks who haven't communicated with you in a while. The problem is that it's an infinite circle of wasted time, and by the time you finish, you forget how far you went with the project. Also, it's a cycle that's impossible to break out of.

When you are attempting to focus, cell phones may be distracting and seem like someone is hitting you over the head. Put an end to it. Put them to use without letting themselves be used by you. You shouldn't make them into an excuse not to get anything done. You may have a peek around noon. You may check during your break for coffee, but other than that, you should make sure that you have a message for those who call and that you urge them to leave messages that you can deal with when you have the time. For instance, your wife could send you a short message reminding you to pick up the dry washing, and you wouldn't have to wait around for a half an hour while she filled you in on what's been going on in her day. Is it a significant day for her? Obviously, it is, but not to the extent that you should allow it to prevent you from completing the tasks that you have to carry out. If you fill your mind with the things that you have to do, there won't be much room for creativity, and it's this creativity that will get everything done when it needs to be done. If you clutter your mind with things that you have to do.

Electronic mail

I used to think of emails as somewhat of an oddity. When I woke up in the morning, the first thing I did was glance at that stack of emails, and then I would proceed to answer those emails for many hours without really giving much thought to what I was doing. You are not able to make the most of your email conversations since your mind is not in the right state first thing in the morning. In addition to this, if you deal with your email first thing in the morning, you take a significant amount of planning out of your mind and allow all of those emails prevent you from getting on with the task at hand. Put them off until after your break for coffee. Consider the time you spend on breaks as an opportunity to recharge your batteries and get caught up. You will discover that you are unable to focus when you allow email to take control of your time because there is too much mental clutter in your mind about the responses that you will provide to the emails that you have received. To avoid this problem, avoid letting email take control of your time. Install an automated reply system. You won't have to let all of the ideas to make your brain feel cluttered if you do it this way. Even just taking a quick glance at the emails might have the same effect. Ignore them entirely. They don't come into existence until we take a break.

The Importance Of Managing Time Effectively

Time management is the ability to plan and direct how you spend the 24 hours in a day in order to successfully accomplish the goals you have set for yourself. The behaviour of delaying, in addition to problems with constraint, may be an indicator of ineffective time management. Managing your time effectively requires a number of skills, such as being able to see forward into the future, establishing goals, planning out errands, and paying attention to how your time is really spent.

Get yourself organised in order to be creative.

People are not born organised; they must develop their organisational skills through time. They need to cultivate dependable habits, which will afterwards assist them in maintaining their organisation. You may carry out your task in the right manner and finish everything without a hitch; but, this is not the objective. The fact of the issue is that you will become better if you have outstanding authoritative attitudes. This is a fact that cannot be denied. Representatives that have this mindset are more productive at work, have a better influence on their managers, and are promoted more often than those whose work habits are characterised by disorganisation and waste. You are also less likely to make careless mistakes or to skip an important appointment, both of which have the potential to severely damage your professional reputation. You wouldn't want it to come about as a consequence of a few indiscreet errors, would you?

Having better time management skills comes hand in hand with increased organisational capacity.

You waste time going through old communications and records to discover missing data or looking for documents and reports that have been misplaced.

You waste time as well by switching between devices in order to receive different kinds of information from different locations.

Be conscious of this, and begin organising and keeping items that you will need in the future in a way that makes them easily accessible right now so that you can make your life easier in the future. It is possible for you to get an increase in productivity while also lowering your stress level and saving time throughout the week.

Do you have any idea how much time you waste looking for something as simple as a piece of paper?

Imagine that you spend around a quarter of a minute out of each hour looking for a piece of paper. If you were to work it out every day, it would take up twelve minutes of your time. At the moment, 12 minutes is not a significant measure, but in the event that you make sense of this every year, then you will be wasting 73 hours of your time. That amounts to more than three days of your life spent doing nothing except looking for a scrap of paper.

Investing Appropriate Time and Energy

If you want to get more done in less time, you need to find out how to properly manage your activities. Being organised is one method to save time, but if you want to get even more done, you need to figure out how to manage your projects. When everything is taken into consideration, the first step in the process of becoming more helpful is to have an awareness of where your time is going at this moment.

Even though the majority of managers are aware in their heads that time is their most valuable resource, relatively few of them make an effort to get an insightful perspective on how they use their waking hours each week. Even fewer people make it a regular habit to track the degree to which the demands they claim are most important match with the ways in which they really devote their time and effort. Those individuals who we consider to be natural-born pioneers and leaders are truly aware of how to exert influence over their historical period.

Putting our efforts towards improving oneself has a lot of different potential benefits. It relieves tension, broadens our perspective on life, and assists us in becoming more self-reliant all at the same time. In addition to this, it elucidates, rationalises, and defines things for us. We are able to steer clear of the pointless dramatisations that are occurring all around us if we focus more of our efforts on improving ourselves.

A wretched existence is certain if we subject ourselves to dreck like harmful relationships and unpleasant chatter.

A growing number of people find that staring at the television is both a relaxing activity and a compulsive habit. All of that time may be used towards something that would be more valuable to one's life or more pleasant, like reading.

Reading will assist you in getting to know and understand the people in your immediate environment, as well as the world and yourself.

A priority in our life should always be given to our families. They are the driving force behind the vast majority of our life choices. Spending time with your loved ones gives you the opportunity to appreciate the most important aspects of life.

Principal Aim

The effective management of one's time may be helpful and rewarding, and it may even be more advantageous than any other aspect of one's life. There must to be a primary objective in life, and in order to accomplish that objective, you should stay on top of things to ensure that they are finished. Getting things done in a timely manner will lead to an increase in the amount of success you experience. While you are working towards a certain objective, it is important that you never lose sight of what it feels like to do tasks at the precise moment they should be completed.

You can easily do massive jobs and perform a lot of different things if you manage your to-do list and make sure the chores are completed on time. Abilities to manage one's time well are vital in almost every endeavour one undertakes in life. You need to be able to efficiently manage your time in order to fulfil both your immediate and long-term goals if you are going to be successful in either running a small company or attending school. This is true whether you are the owner of a sole proprietorship or a student.

Having A Good Handle On Time Management

The ability to use your time efficiently is what we mean when we talk about using time effectively. It is the process of planning and organising your whole day in such a way that it enables you to perform all of your responsibilities within the allotted amount of time. It refers to the manner in which you arrange things or plan the activities you engage in.

To put it another way, effective time management is all about striking a balance and maintaining control.

You have to have a good understanding of the meaning of the word "wisely" if you want to become the greatest at utilising time in a productive manner. It teaches you about the what, why, when, and how of many topics. The answers to all of these questions will play a significant part in determining your destiny.

If you look carefully, you'll see that all successful individuals have a good understanding of how to manage their time effectively. They were able to schedule their activities in a productive manner. And this is the reason why they were able to accomplish their objectives in a shorter amount of time.

Learn the art of time management if you want to increase your chances of living the life of your dreams. You just need this one ability to simplify everything in your life and put you on the path to success.

In order to effectively manage time, it is not enough to just divide your day into 24 equal parts; you must also choose the amount of time you will devote to each task. It is one of those talents that assists in deciding what time to set for whatever activity in order to bring about riches.

Learning how to effectively manage one's time is a crucial component for the task at hand since it enables one to construct a solid foundation. If your foundation is sturdy enough, you will be able to sculpt almost any building. Even doing so will give you a feeling of accomplishment and inspire you to do great things in life.

The realisation that you have control over your time and can use it well may bring a sense of calm and contentment into your life. Additionally, it assists in the reduction of stress, the improvement of productivity, the maintenance of a healthy work-life balance, and the instillation of a feeling of control over one's life.

* * *

You need to be able to wait, as I said before, since achieving achievement takes time. You only need to make sure that your life is well-planned and well-organized in order for it to provide you the greatest outcomes possible. If you devote all of your energy to the task that produces positive results, you will be one step closer to establishing a reputation for yourself in the global community.

You may make the most of the time you have available by making use of a variety of tactics for time management. Setting priorities, maintaining a to-do list, utilising a planner or calendar, keeping a to-do list, and using different time management tools are some of the things that might help you remain on track.

Keep in mind that making effective use of your time does not need you to spend the whole of each day micromanaging your responsibilities. It would be unethical and have a negative effect on you. It is even possible that it may cause you stress. Instead, take some time for yourself to unwind, and only after that should you go on to the next phase of planning. Maintaining your composure as you plan will help you come up with the best strategy for moving forward. It will make the procedure much easier for you.

Is Your Freedom In Danger When You Have a Deadline to Meet?

If you have been working without a deadline, the thought of having one may leave you with a sour taste in your mouth.

You absolutely do not want to establish a beginning time and an end time for this. You may begin whenever you choose, and you can continue and complete it in whichever manner best suits your whims and desires.

The sensation of having this independence is intoxicating. However, unless you labour for pleasure or to kill time, you won't accomplish much by doing so.

If you don't give yourself deadlines for your tasks, it's possible that you'll never complete the majority of them. Why? because there is no pressing need to do so at this time.

The longer you work on a project, the more probable it is that you will lose interest in it as time goes on.

There must be some initiatives that you've given up on because you didn't have a clear idea of when to begin and when to end them.

A lot of people are looking for the key to increased productivity, but they don't realise that it's only one word: dateline.

When working under a time constraint, you immediately become more concentrated and rush towards achieving your objective. You speed up to a full-out run in the last stretch of the race.

Therefore, you should look on the bright side of having deadlines. There is a greater number of positives than negatives.

The primary advantage is that once you get used to the concept of deadlines, you will see an automatic increase in your level of productivity.

The Craft of Establishing Due Dates

Keep your sights set on a goal that can be attained.

When establishing timelines, you really have to have a goal in mind. The objective of a football game that is played for three quarters of an hour is to score goals.

Everyone works together to reach that goal, and they make the most of every chance to do so.

Therefore, when you are setting a deadline, you need to be sure that your aim is extremely defined. Aim towards the centre of the target.

Let's say you've decided to write a fresh piece for your site. You are aware that you cannot complete it in a single sitting. First, you'll create an outline, then a first draught, then do research, and last, you'll revise the piece before publishing it.

You are responsible for four different things in this area. Imagine if you only post once every three days.

Let's say you want to begin by creating an outline. If you just begin outlining without setting any time markers, you may find that the process never ends. If things don't start to go your way, you could even be tempted to mix it with research and find yourself falling into a rabbit hole as a result.

So, what are you going to do? During the process of outlining, you decide to establish a time restriction for yourself, say twenty minutes. You have no more than twenty minutes to complete the blueprint before moving on to the next step. During this time, you are not permitted to engage in any other activities.

Therefore, even if your outlining is unsuccessful, you will only have thrown away a total of twenty minutes of your time. It's not a huge problem.

You will have the opportunity to attempt it once again at a later time. Time is not lost. Energy that was saved. Gain made through transparency.

Continue on to the next undertaking, irrespective of the results of the previous one.

Begin with a manageable chunk of the project if the pressure of impending deadlines continues to get to you.

You may want to consider outlining three things that you want to discuss in the opening of the blog article before you publish it. The time limit has been set at 10 minutes. You should give it a go.

Once again, begin with the mindset of "I've got nothing to lose" by setting a short (mini) timeframe for yourself to work inside.

You are teaching yourself to complete tasks within the allotted time. Begin on a low scale. Make some headway. Your spirits will rise as soon as you get moving and quit wasting time, so get going. Naturally, you'll find yourself wanting to put in more effort.

Productivity-Boosting Patterns You Should Adopt

The overwhelming majority of people have the experience of feeling as if they are not sufficiently productive in their day-to-day lives. They fall short of accomplishing all of the objectives they have set for themselves, whether it is at job, in their personal life, or in the realm of their social lives. This low level of production can almost always be traced back to either a paucity of time or energy, or perhaps even a combination of the two. It's a shame there isn't a wand or a potion that can conjure up additional time or energy out of thin air, but there isn't one. On the other hand, increasing production does not require breaking any physical rules since there are alternative methods available. After all, the most successful individuals in life are those who are able to do what they set out to do in the same twenty-four hour period that the typical person gets to work with. The key is to develop routines that enable a person to realise their full potential for productivity. In this chapter, you will learn about five of the most productive habits that will help you to become more productive in your everyday life by making better use of the time and energy that you currently have available to you.

The first routine you should establish is a daily one.

The creation of a daily routine is one of the most essential practises that all successful individuals incorporate into their day-to-day life. Successful people do this because they recognise its significance. They are aware that although it is impossible to add more time to a given day, it is possible to make more efficient use of the time one already has. You may limit the amount of time that is lost during the day by organising your schedule, which will provide you with the resources you need to complete all of the tasks at hand.

Your daily routine ought to include each and every facet of your day. Your wake-up time and the time you turn in for the night should be consistent from day to day. The time at which you consume your meals as well as the amount of time you spend doing so should be consistent. Essentially, you will need to devise a timetable that you will adhere to in order to make sure that everything has its proper home. When it comes to being disciplined with the time you have, having such a timetable can allow you to boost your ability to do so.

Create a To-Do List Every Day as Your Second Daily Habit

Creating a list of the things that need to be done each day is another practise that highly successful individuals do in each and every day. This list fulfils two very separate purposes. To begin, it brings all of the critical activities to your attention, which makes it easier for you to remember them and keeps you motivated over the course of the day. You may cross each item off your list as you do it, which will make it easier for you to monitor how far along you are during the day.

The second advantage of maintaining a task list is that it prevents you from taking on too many responsibilities all at once. When you don't have a task list to refer to, it may be all too simple to add more and more work to your agenda. This can be a problem since the list would show you how busy your day already is. However, if you are aware that you already have a full schedule for the day, you are in a better position to politely decline extra responsibilities that can cause you to get overworked and, as a result, reduce your level of productivity.

Take Care of the Most Important Obligations First

while it comes to increasing your productivity, one of the best kept secrets is to tackle the most difficult assignments while you have the greatest energy available to devote to them. Because of the fact that a person's energy levels are often strongest in the morning, it is recommended that significant responsibilities be tackled as soon as possible in the day rather than being pushed off until later. You can guarantee that you will have the energy you need to do the significant duties at the beginning of the day, which will allow you to complete them as swiftly and simply as is humanly feasible.

The remainder of the day will be far less taxing on your mental capacity if you start the day by handling the more difficult activities. Therefore, rather of your day being tougher and harder as time continues, it will actually become easier, leaving you feeling wonderful at the end of the day rather than fatigued like the ordinary person would feel after a typical day.

Eliminating Distractions Is the Fourth Habit.

Eliminating distractions may be the single most significant practise for recuperating lost time, and it is certainly one of the most time-efficient. In this day and age of smartphones and applications of all sorts and sizes, it may be all too tempting to spend five or ten minutes catching up on social media, reading emails, playing a brief game, or even simply messaging friends and loved ones. However, it is important to remember that these activities should not be prioritised over more important tasks. Unfortuitously, these little snippets of time mount up over the course of a day, which results in hours of time that cannot be recovered. It is essential that you get rid of any and all distractions if you want to prevent wasting time and resources like this.

In this regard, the most essential move you can do is to mute or turn off the sound on your mobile device. However, shutting off other potential distractions, such as televisions, radios, and other similar devices, may also assist you in maintaining your concentration on the work at hand. Talk radio may be quite distracting when working, while music can be calming when played in the background. Eliminate anything, then, that has the potential to lead you to divert your focus away from the activity that you are attempting to do.

Take plenty of breaks, as recommended in Habit No. 5

It is really ironic that one of the greatest methods to boost productivity is, in fact, to take more breaks; this has been shown by a number of studies to be one of the best approaches. A person's attention has a tendency to wander when they are fatigued, and their energy levels begin to decrease when they are exhausted. This is the bottom line. This only becomes worse as the person progresses from being weary to exhausted and worn out. The most effective approach to prevent this is to schedule a number of short breaks throughout the day and stick to them religiously.

A great method to get your thoughts organised before moving on to the next assignment is to give yourself a little break of 10 minutes between each one. A little stretch of the legs at this time will also assist to start the blood flowing, which will maintain your levels of energy higher all throughout the day, so allowing you to do more tasks as a direct consequence of this.

www.ingramcontent.com/pod-product-compliance
Lightning Source LLC
Chambersburg PA
CBHW050232120526
44590CB00016B/2053